Tempomatic IV

Tempomatic IV
A Management Simulation

Third Edition

Charles R. Scott, Jr.
University of Alabama

Alonzo J. Strickland III
University of Alabama

HOUGHTON MIFFLIN COMPANY • BOSTON

Dallas • Geneva, Illinois • Hopewell, New Jersey • Palo Alto

Printed in the U.S.A.

Library of Congress Catalog Card Number: 79-89182

ISBN: 0-395-34299-6

HIJ-M-9654321

Contents

Preface

Some twenty-five years ago, schools of business administration began accelerating their search for innovative teaching methods; this search, with consequent adoptions and adaptations, has resulted in curricula that embody a new diversity of methodology. The new methodology focuses not exclusively on the descriptive content of the contributing disciplines but on their interrelationships as well. The study of business, therefore, becomes the study of these interrelationships: the study of an organization as a system within other systems and of the functional areas of an organization as they relate to one another. This new methodology also takes into account the changing nature of the students, emphasizing productive interactions among inquiring, critical, participating persons.

One of the products of this evolution in teaching is the business "game," or business management simulation. As a teaching device it allows participants to integrate and apply their accumulated knowledge using a systems approach to master the skills of decision making, and to function as managers in a simulated but realistic business environment.

TEMPOMATIC was originally conceived and designed in 1959 as a hand-computed management game. In the early 1960s TEMPOMATIC was programmed for the computer. Since then, improvements, additions, and refinements have been made in the simulation and its program, resulting in the third edition of TEMPOMATIC IV. Special efforts have been directed toward making TEMPOMATIC realistic, keeping it focused on current management issues, eliminating computer bugs and the need for computer ability on the part of the game administrator, realistically dealing with student innovation, and providing the students and the administrator with helpful information. The simulation has been designed to balance realism with complexity. The required number of decisions has been kept to a reasonable level for initial and subsequent stages of play. The third edition of TEMPOMATIC IV has expanded the instructor's capability to add complexity to the decision making as desired. For example, the simulation now allows for changes to be made in company productivity and crew size for production workers, overhead rate, and salesperson's salary and hiring cost; to invest in new technology for existing plant and equipment; to lay off production workers; and to carry income losses back one calendar year or forward one calendar year. Additional instructor reports have been added to summarize every aspect of the industry. The administrator now has the ability to create a bull or bear market for stock issuances, to allow sales to be above projected forecasts when market emphasis is strong, and to vary plant construction costs by area. Special emphasis has kept the decision making balanced among the various areas.

The third edition of TEMPOMATIC IV is programmed to provide participants with computer output on added financial and other information. The printed output has been revised for greater clarity and improved participant analyses.

Students are innovative, and they should be encouraged to be so. They devise methods to beat the simulation and try to out-guess the computer model. Some of the students' innovative thinking is reflected in the revisions of the computer program, and the simulation is better for this testing. Moreover, the quality of the decision making seems to assume the character of the participants each time the simulation is played; the administrator can keep this in mind when choosing the environment within which the simulation will be played. Thus TEMPOMATIC continues to change and improve.

TEMPOMATIC IV is primarily a tool for teaching decision making within a compact time frame; although it is self-regulating, it can be adjusted by the administrator to fit the needs of the course. It has been tested tens of thousands of times in numerous ways and is now in its fourth generation of growth.

In revising the TEMPOMATIC IV student manual, we have clarified and rearranged material, updated wage levels, and included cost/benefit analysis opportunities by allowing productivity and crew size to be variable on a company by company basis. In addition, technological improvements can be made to the plants to allow them to be more efficient. The Instructor's Manual has been thoroughly revised to make it more useful to instructors who are using a simulation for the first time. And, as in the first edition, a Computer Center Manual assists in interfacing with the computer center. The various changes made for the third edition should help participants better understand the complex information needed for the game, assist the administrator with productive teaching information, and, overall, clearly emphasize the application of management processes to business situations.

A special option for this edition of TEMPOMATIC IV is a tempomatic planning model using the well known VisiCalc software. All information needed to use the model is found in Appendix C.

The real credit for the third edition rests with the many adopters around the country who have made suggestions for improving TEMPOMATIC IV. Of course, any errors in this edition are the sole responsibility of the authors.

C.R.S.
A.J.S.

Introduction

The effective business executive understands the performance of a business organization in the economy and understands the character of decisions to be made. This understanding accrues from years of study and experience. You as students of business are acquiring knowledge through formal courses using lectures, discussions, and case study, through professional reading, through work experience, and through conferences and seminars. Each of these means of gaining the knowledge and analytical ability required to understand the overall working of a company has its limitations. Limitations on time, on content and breadth of study, and on coordination lead you to look for something to connect, relate, and fuse the facts you have mastered to form a total body of knowledge.

This business management simulation, TEMPOMATIC IV, is designed to help you bring together all areas of your present knowledge and to give you experience in the use of theories and techniques required in the business world. It allows you to participate in decision making without entering the real-life activity. Just as men in the space shuttle program first "flew the shuttle" through space-flight simulation, you too, through this business management simulation, can learn how to "run a company" competitively under a given set of economic conditions. The simulation requires you as participants to make decisions in all functional areas of a business and requires you to search for the appropriate theories and techniques to use in your decision making. It places the company in a specified economic setting and compresses the company's activities so that several years of endeavor may be simulated in a few hours of work.

A business simulation is based on certain relationships among the various functioning parts of the given business unit and is enacted by the participants who make decisions, the game administrator who uses predetermined relationships to assess group performance, and the participants who evaluate the results for the next set of decisions. Each participant is assigned to a company which competes with other companies in an environment similar to that of real business.

The actions of competitors and the making of decisions based on results of one's past decisions differentiate the simulation from case analysis. It is as some participants have said: "You live with your past decisions and every other company's decisions." If you as a participant enter enthusiastically into the activities of this simulation, you will find ready use for much of the knowledge you have acquired from your previous studies and you will gain experience that will contribute to your future expertise as a business manager.

THE TEMPOMATIC IV LEARNING EXPERIENCE

TEMPOMATIC IV is not planned for any specific product or industry. This vagueness is intentional and precludes the participants' decisions begin based on the known actions of any real company. TEMPOMATIC IV has been developed to afford students a planned, systematic learning experience in integrating knowledge acquired in modern business schools. Aiding in this attempt are the instructor, who plays many roles from management consultant to labor representative; this manual, which explores in detail the rules and options of TEMPOMATIC IV; and the model itself, which consists of a computer program capable of being handled on most modern computer systems. However, the student need have no knowledge of computer capability.

Briefly the management simulation cycle is as follows. First, participants gain an understanding of the simulated environment in which they are to operate from the information presented in this manual and possibly from discussions of the manual in class. Then companies are formed, all of which will compete with one product, TEMPOMATIC, in three market areas. Participants are assigned to manage the individual companies, each of which is patterned on the one company described in this manual. Each management team then studies the operating statements furnished by the previous management of its company and makes a set of decisions.

At the beginning all companies are exactly alike, in order to eliminate any question of favoritism. After each management team has entered its decisions on a decision sheet, the decisions are submitted at an announced time to the TEMPOMATIC IV administrator for processing. The decisions are analyzed by the TEMPOMATIC IV computer program, and new sets of operating statements for the company are generated and returned to the respective teams. The teams consult with the instructor at intervals for negotiation of the terms of loans, wages, and other business transactions, for presentation of reports, and for evaluation of team progress. This cycle of making analyses and decisions, seeking results, and then making more decisions continues for a specified number of periods, designated as quarters.

OBJECTIVES OF TEMPOMATIC IV

TEMPOMATIC IV can be as simple or as complex as the business knowledge of the player. For the beginning student, whose knowledge of techniques is rather basic, the level of the game can be fairly simple. The senior student can use more complex techniques for decision making, and thereby increase the complexity of the game.

At the graduate level, students are expected to have knowledge of quantitative decision making, including stochastic models, present-value analysis, information systems, linear programming, and many other highly sophisticated techniques. For the businessperson, TEMPOMATIC IV can be conducted at a simple or a complex level as conditions dictate. Moreover, since the teams themselves set the competitive environment, no optimum solution exists. Each play of the simulation is different, and the results will vary greatly depending on the background and level of the players. The game literally takes on their personalities.

TEMPOMATIC IV offers many opportunities and situations for applying numerous modern decision making techniques. Students compete with each other and not with the computer. Players of TEMPOMATIC IV learn, also through practice, the importance of integrating operating schedules and reports in a logical manner in order to make sound decisions. They learn rapidly that they can reduce their total decision making time by keeping records and reports conscientiously. The benefit of proper utilization of an information system is learned through practice.

TEMPOMATIC IV is unique in that it represents all the functional areas of a complete business entity. Since production, marketing, and finance functions exist in the simulation, the players face the real problems of allocating resources. They learn very quickly that they must coordinate the functions and that they may not reach their predetermined goals if any function is maximized at the expense of the others.

While studying decision tools such as profit-volume analysis, students ordinarily do not have the opportunity to gather data for their models or to use their findings to make decisions. Using profit-volume analysis in the simulation, students learn that locating fixed and variable costs is not as easy as they might at first have thought and that having more data than are needed can present additional problems. The simulation provides the participants with conditions under which they must decide which tool is appropriate in making a specific decision.

Finally, the decisions in each period of the simulation are influenced by what has happened in the past and forecasts of what will happen in the future. Because of this, each team must learn to live with previous decisions, good and bad. The advisability of changing a plan even after one has committed oneself becomes apparent especially when a series of bad decisions has been made. The fact that the players constantly face a deadline makes for a realistic decision making environment.

You and the Company

You and several other new managers have been hired for management positions in a simulated company—the Gidget Company—described throughout the rest of this manual. Your job as a manager is to allocate your company's resources to the best advantage. You compete directly with the other companies in your industry, and accordingly, the decisions of competitive firms affect Gidget's performance.

The stockholders of the Gidget Company have been dissatisfied with the results of previous management's policies and decisions and have asked your management team to take over. At the same time, the stockholders of your competitors have become dissatisfied with the management of their companies too. In fact, a very highly improbable thing has happened: all the companies have the same history, are starting at the same point, and sell the same product in the same market. We can therefore say that the history and the present situation of the Gidget Company are representative of all the other companies in the industry.

COMPANY HISTORY

A.W. Gidget used to work for a small retail business selling small consumer durable goods, but he was more interested in inventing new devices and he really wanted to have his own business. About four years ago he invented TEMPOMATIC, a product that can be classed with others he was selling, including clock radios, blenders, toasters, and small tape recorders. Since he did not have much money, he took his invention to several of his friends who might be interested in investing in making and marketing TEMPOMATICs and who could provide the necessary financial backing. His friends were indeed interested. They made a preliminary survey to determine the market forecast of TEMPOMATICs and an analysis of the production methods and costs that would be necessary.

Three years ago a corporation was formed with Mr. Gidget and other stockholders owning a total of 100,000 shares of common stock valued at $10 per share. The company decided that, instead of doing all the manufacturing itself, it would buy kits (raw material) and assemble the material to make TEMPOMATICs. The market survey indicated that the company should start marketing with plant and offices as shown in the circle in Figure 2.1, with possible additions depending on growth. When the company had been formed, it was named after Mr. Gidget, the inventor of its product, and he became its first president.

The company then searched for a plant, ordered the machinery and equipment, and placed advertisements for production workers and salespersons. A building was found in the community, the machinery was installed, and production and sales personnel were hired. The

FIGURE 2.1 *Overview of Tempomatic IV*

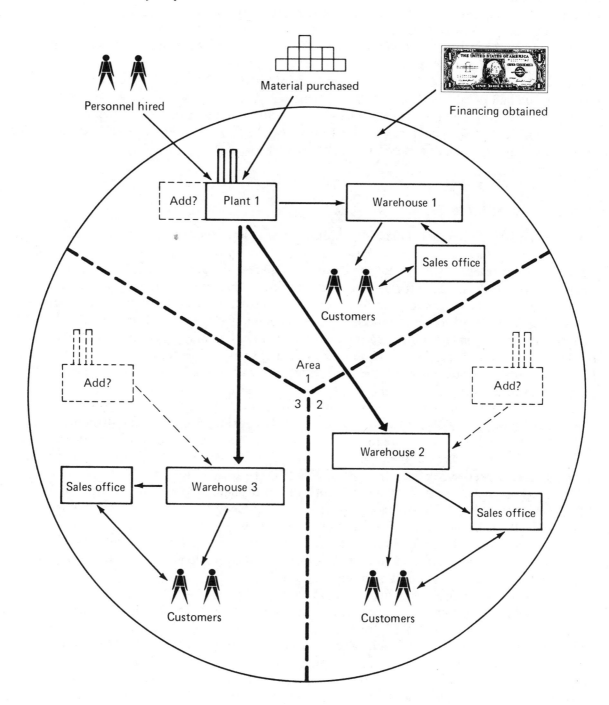

current operation and the plans for expansion are as shown in Figure 2.1. The kits (raw material) are assembled into TEMPOMATICs at Plant 1 by crews of three production workers; the products are sold by salespersons working out of nearby offices. Since the company was small to begin with, all the major decisions and analyses were made by a team of three managers at the plant office in Area 1.

After about a year, Mr. Gidget relinquished the presidency to devote his time to new inventions he had developed, and a new president was hired. Since then, the company has had the same management, and the results of its decisions are reported in the operating statements described and illustrated in Chapter 3. Figure 2.2 shows changes in several indicators of the company's financial position during the past two years.

COMPANY POLICIES

The elected board of directors of the Gidget Company has established some important guidelines for the incoming management team during the next three to four years. The directors do not want to expend resources to expand the company's market beyond the circle in Figure 2.1. They feel that the demand for the product is expanding in this market and they want management to exploit it. The company sells its product by improving the product image of TEMPO-MATICs and by the efforts of salespersons, who are supported with two forms of advertising. The previous management considered the use of wholesalers, retailers, and mail-order outlets, but the board decided that the use of retailers utilizing salespersons would be more effective. The market characteristics of each of the three territories or areas differ. Salespersons assigned to an area and local advertising bought in that area affect sales only in that area.

Some advertising and improvements in the product affect the total market, however. The Gidget Company has maintained in the past a policy of one sales price, even though transporting TEMPOMATICs from area to area increases costs. The market characteristics have precluded asking higher prices in the higher-cost areas, but this has not stopped the company from making market-wide price increases of TEMPOMATICs in the past.

The previous management proposed the integration of manufacture and assembly of TEMPOMATICs. It considered buying its suppliers in order either to incorporate the suppliers' profits with those of the Gidget Company or to reduce the price of TEMPOMATICs. The board members decided that the money that would be required would be better spent expanding the company's assembly facilities to take care of the expanding demand. Demand has grown during the eight quarters since Mr. Gidget relinquished the presidency.

The company has twice expanded the capacity of its Area 1 plant; the second expansion required the hiring of twenty-four new production workers and was completed in time for scheduling the assembly of TEMPOMATICs in this past quarter. The company has had few problems hiring new employees, but it has had a high turnover rate and has been faced with some rigid labor practices. The turnover rate is comparable to that of the other businesses in the community. The assembly of kits requires semi-skilled employees, and the character of the assembly process demands a specific crew size. To reduce the crew size the company would have had to invest in expensive equipment, and it would also have had to change the precedent that has been established in the industry. The board members have decided to accept these constraints for the present.

The company has had until now only one supplier of kits. It has not been able to interest other suppliers because of technical problems in the manufacture of the kits, and the Gidget Company does not buy enough kits to make it worth other suppliers' time to redesign and manufacture them. The quality of the present supplier has been excellent, however; the price of the kits, even with one increase, is reasonable; and the delivery of orders has been good.

FIGURE 2.2 *Past Operating Curves*

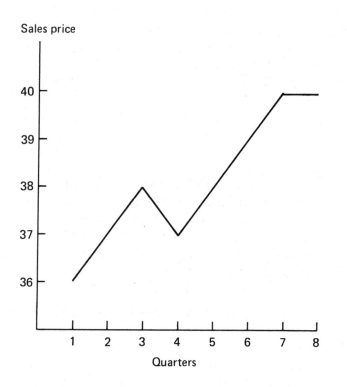

Sales price

Quarters

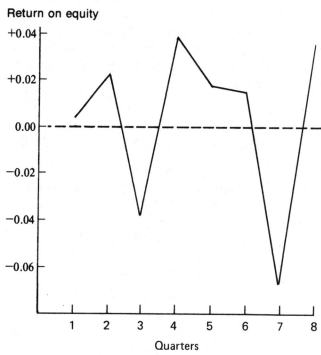

Return on equity

Quarters

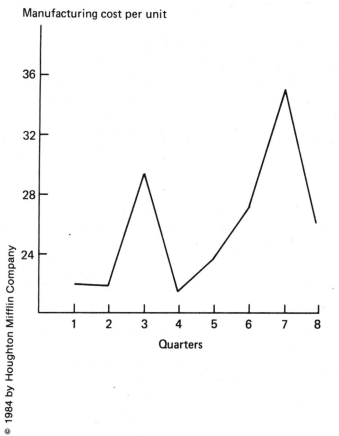

Manufacturing cost per unit

Quarters

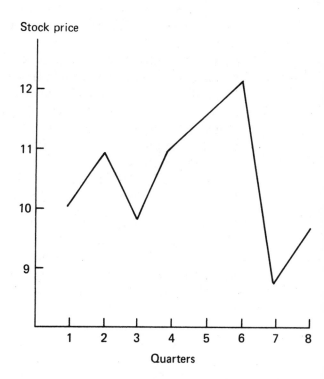

Stock price

Quarters

The Gidget Company was financed initially through subscriptions to shares of stock. Equity has since increased, and a long-term indebtedness has been incurred in the form of two bond issues, short-term notes, and taxes payable (see the financial statements for quarter 8 in Appendix B). The company has good relations with the financial institutions with which it does business; thus, money can be obtained reasonably easily. The company has had high accounts receivable because the industry has very lax cash-payment practices, with only 10 percent being collected in the quarter sold. There have been attempts to tighten up, but they have had negative results. The board of directors has agreed that the company will have to follow current policy.

YOU AND COMPANY MANAGEMENT

Your management team is to make decisions in the same areas as the past management, but the board members expect better results from you. In the past, there has seemed to be little firm direction, and the decisions to change were initiated slowly and erratically. You are limited by the policies and rules of your board of directors, just as the past management was, but you still have considerable latitude in your decision making. Following is a list of questions indicating the types of decisions you will need to make. All the decisions of your management team will be based on your ideas for the allocation of resources.

1. How should your team organize for most effective managing and what are your objectives and strategies?
2. How much should you spend on obtaining information about the future market, your competitors' activities, and miscellaneous environmental activities of the future?
3. How much sales promotion should you have and how should it be allocated? How do these allocations relate to the sales price you choose? Would a new name for the company be beneficial?
4. How many units should you produce, how much material should you order, how many employees should you hire, and where should you warehouse your TEMPOMATICs? Certainly your decisions should include analyses of the levels of your inventories.
5. How large a production capacity should you have, and where should it be located? How should you handle variable demand?
6. How should you obtain and distribute additional funds? How should you distribute the company's earnings?
7. How should you handle the demands of the union that represents your workers? What should you do if your workers threaten to strike?

These questions indicate your role during your management tenure. They do not indicate all the decisions you will make, nor do they indicate the frequency of the need for decision making. Subsequent chapters provide a detailed discussion of decision problems and their character. You will notice that some decisions, such as those regarding plant construction, occur infrequently but that others, such as the problems in hiring personnel, occur each period.

Many of the people who normally interact with a company will not be available during the play of the game; the simulation administrator will fill their roles. The simulation administrator may be, in turn, an instructor to help you learn the game and how to manage, a banker or broker as a negotiator for money, a union leader in negotiations over wages, and a board member to help set policies and rules.

You may already have observed some current inflexible rules such as the one-price policy and the fixed crew size. This inflexibility is to protect you at the start of the game. If you had to make all the decisions of an ongoing company—that is, if the simulation were too realistic—you would not in the time allotted be able to cope with so many variables. Very complex games admitting real-life variability tend to develop into gambling situations at the expense of analytical decision making. However, as the simulation progresses, some of the rules may be relaxed. You will be given advance notice of these changes.

3

The Environment and Your Company

All the companies in the TEMPOMATIC industry sell in the same market. This chapter presents the nature of that market and the details of the internal operations of Gidget, the representative company. Each quarter, Gidget is furnished by its accountants with a series of operating statements, including statements of production analysis, manufacturing cost of goods sold, warehouse operations, selling and administrative expense analysis, cash flow, income, and financial position. It is imperative that you understand the information each statement provides. All the statements are presented in Appendix B and described in detail in the following pages. Your starting statements pertain to quarter 8, and it is recommended that you remove the quarter 8 statements from the Appendix and keep them beside the text as you read this chapter.

THE MARKET

The market for the industry in each of the three areas shown in Figure 2.1 is determined by the sum of the sales forecasts for the industry's companies with adjustments indicated below. Table 3.1 shows the per company actual sales for quarters 1 through 8, and the simulation administrator will provide you with the per company sales forecasts for quarters 9 through 12. To compute the sum of the sales forecasts for the total market for each area, multiply the forecast in the area by the number of companies in the industry. For example, in quarter 8 with an industry of three companies, the sales forecast was 22,500 ($3 \times 7,500$) units in Area 1, 16,800 ($3 \times 5,600$) units in Area 2, and 15,000 ($3 \times 5,000$) units in Area 3—a total of 54,300 units in all three areas.

Market forecasts are forecasts of the volume of sales expected under certain conditions of the economy and with certain sales efforts of the companies in the industry. Lack of sales effort or extraordinary sales effort in an area influences the industry sales in that area. Past sales of TEMPOMATICs have moved away from the forecasts when the economic conditions deviated from the forecasted conditions. The movement of the Business Week Index (BWI) has been a good measure of this deviation, so in the future the forecasts will be adjusted for changes in the BWI. The BWI at the time of initiation of play (quarter 9) will be used as the base point for future changes. As the BWI increases, so will the forecast and vice versa; however, the exact relationship between the BWI and the forecast is not available except to say they move in the same direction.

The share of the market that your company obtains depends on your sales effort relative to the sales efforts of other companies in the industry as well as the total industry sales effort. If your area sales effort is greater than the average in the industry, your area sales will be greater than the average as long as you have enough units available to sell. Sales effort depends on your company's product price, the number of salespersons, the number of pages of advertising that it buys, and the number of product improvements that it makes. Thus your sales in each area depend on the size of the total market and on your sales effort in relation to that of the rest of the industry in that area. You will be wise to keep informed on the activities in the market and in the industry.

In addition, if the industry as a whole fails to have enough sales effort, the total market can shrink as substitute goods come into the market. For example, if we consider TEMPOMATICs to be clock radios, then as the price of the radios increases without a corresponding amount of a combination of national and local advertising, salespersons, and/or product improvements on the part of the industry, customers will shift to other means of waking up in the morning, such as inexpensive electric clocks and transistor radios.

On the other hand, if the industry as a whole has a substantial amount of sales effort, it is possible for the total demand to increase. You should anticipate, however, that the increase in sales due to sales effort or a decrease in sales due to a lack of sales effort will not typically affect the sales more than 15 percent. The exact switching costs are not available.

TABLE 3.1 *Unit Sales Forecast, Quarters 1–12*

| Quarter | Area Sales Potential | | | |
	1	2	3	Total
1	6,200	4,200	2,300	12,700
2	6,100	4,100	2,200	12,400
3	6,400	4,400	2,400	13,200
4	6,800	4,700	3,100	14,600
5	7,100	4,900	3,300	15,300
6	6,700	5,200	4,000	15,900
7	7,000	5,100	4,300	16,400
8	7,500	5,600	5,000	18,100

	Sales Forecast[a]			
9				
10				
11				
12				

[a]Obtained from Environment Information Form. Will be provided by administrator.

PRODUCTION ANALYSIS

Purchasing and Inventory of Kits

The production analysis statement details your inventories of kits (raw material) and your labor forces in the three operational areas.

Kits of raw material are purchased and assembled into finished products at the rate of one kit per finished product. Delivery time for raw material is one quarter, and therefore material (kits) must be ordered one quarter ahead of use. The present prices are in effect for quarter 9 but are subject to change in the future:

Number of Kits	Price per Kit
1 to 9,999	$10
10,000 to 19,999	$9
20,000 and over	$8

Since each area is independent, quantity discounts apply only within an area and not for the total of the areas. For example, if you order 12,000 kits each for Area 1 and Area 2, making a total of 24,000 kits, the price will still be $9 per kit.

In quarter 8, you have a beginning inventory of 1,600 units valued at $10,812 in Area 1. As you can see in the statement, Areas 2 and 3 have no inventories. During quarter 8, you received 20,000 units (kits) that had been ordered the previous quarter. Thus you have available 21,600 units in all. You used 18,000 units in quarter 8 producing TEMPOMATICs, so you have a final inventory of 3,600 valued at $28,379 which is reflected on your balance sheet. In your decision for quarter 8 you ordered an additional 20,000 units that will be received in quarter 9. Thus at the beginning of quarter 9 you will have 23,600 units available for production. Because of supplier and transportation problems there is a 7 percent probability in effect each quarter for each area that only 80 percent of the units in an order will arrive. The units lost can be recovered only by reordering them.

There is a carrying cost associated with the raw material inventory; to compute it, multiply $1 by your beginning inventory. For quarter 8, you had a beginning inventory of 1,600 units, so the carrying cost is $1 × 1,600, or $1,600.

Under the rules of cost accounting, material cost is not recognized until material has been consumed, and therefore the total material cost is the amount used plus the associated carrying cost for the period. The total material cost is then transferred to the statement for manufacturing cost of goods sold.

Work Force

The work force (lines 10-18 on production analysis) is composed of crews of three semi-skilled workers, and there are no partial crews. Each worker is currently being paid the regular wage of $2,500 per quarter; overtime is computed at $15 labor cost per unit. It costs $3,000 plus regular wages to hire a production worker, and workers must be hired one quarter in advance of their first day's labor. If you decide you are going to need 6 new workers in quarter 10, for example, they must be hired in quarter 9. If workers are discharged, the workers will leave at the beginning of the quarter before turnover calculations are made. Workers discharged are shown in line 11. Workers can be laid off at a per worker [per quarter] cost specified by the game administrator. For example, say the layoff cost is $200 and you wish to lay off 5 workers in quarter 10. The workers will be laid off in quarter 10 for a total cost of $1,000. Note that unless the workers are laid off again in quarter 11, the five workers will return automatically at the beginning of quarter 11.

Concerning your present work force, you started quarter 8 with 55 workers (line 10), but you lost 2 due to normal turnover rate of 1 turnover per 20 employees per area. Thus you had available in quarter 8 53 workers. These 53 employees make 17 crews of 3 workers each with 2 workers left over. Notice that in quarter 8 you have made the decision to hire 3 additional employees, which will result in your having 56 employees available at the beginning of quarter 9 (line 10 Next Quarter). Normal turnover in quarter 9 will result in your losing 2 additional workers; therefore, for quarter 9 you will have 54 workers available, or exactly 18 crews of 3 workers each.

In addition to the normal turnover rate of 1 worker per 20, there is a 7 percent probability that you will lose 1 additional worker and a 3 percent probability that you will lose 2 additional workers. Thus, in quarter 9, you could lose up to 4 workers (2 due to normal turnover and 2 due to probabilistic turnover). Since you cannot have a partial crew, the probabilistic turnover should be watched very carefully because it could result in your having fewer crews than you thought, forcing you into an overtime situation. Also remember that because each area is independent of the others, the probabilities are in effect for each area separately.

Each crew is capable of working up to 20 percent overtime. The charge is currently $15 per unit. Using quarter 8 as an example, we see that the 17 crews are able to assemble 17,000 units (17 crews × 1000 unit productivity per crew). The maximum amount of overtime production would be 20 percent of 17,000 or 3,400, for a total of 20,400 units (17,000 plus 3,400). Production without overtime is limited to plant capacity and the number of crews times the productivity rate. Plants, like production crews, are capable of operating at a rate 20 percent above capacity. To assist you in knowing the maximum production that you can accomplish without overtime, line 18 of your production analysis report shows this figure for you. Note that total production is also limited by the kits available in line 3 of your production analysis statement.

Plant

Line 19 in the next statement of production analysis details your plant capacities in the various areas for both this quarter and next and shows the existence in quarter 8 of a plant in Area 1 with an 18,000 unit capacity. You do not have any capacity in the two other areas. Lines 20 and 21 show that you have no plants under construction and that you did not order any new plants in quarter 8.

There are two ways to obtain additional plant capacity; one is to build a new plant, and the other is to buy an existing plant. Moreover, any number of additions may be made to the basic plant in minimum orders of 1,000 units per quarter at a current cost of $100 per unit or a price specified by the administrator. You may construct new plants at a minimum order of 5,000 units also at a current cost of $100 per unit. The 5,000 units means that the plant can assemble 5,000 TEMPOMATICs per quarter. If you build a plant, the payment terms are 20 percent down with the remaining 80 percent due the next quarter. For example, if you decide to build a 6,000 unit plant in quarter 9, $120,000 (.20 × 6000 × $100) will be due in quarter 9, and the remaining $480,000 due in quarter 10. The actual construction of the physical facility takes two quarters, the quarter in which you order and the quarter the plant is under construction. Using the same example from above, the plant is ordered in quarter 9, is under construction in quarter 10, and is ready to be utilized at the beginning of quarter 11.

The procedure is different if you buy an existing plant. First, the purchase price is negotiated with another team or with the game administrator; second, the financing is cash on delivery; and third, the plant comes into production one quarter sooner than if you had built. Assume that in quarter 9 you elect to purchase a 7,000 unit plant for $840,000 (20 percent above the build price). In quarter 9 you would purchase the plant; in quarter 10 you would pay the full $840,000 and the plant would be ready to be utilized. Thus the advantage of purchasing a plant over building it is that you get it one quarter sooner, but you typically pay more. Do not forget that when you either build or purchase a plant you must also hire workers and order raw material.

Later in the game, the game administrator may give you the option of making changes in existing plants that will improve the productivity of your work force and/or changing the number of workers per crew. Typically, the changes in existing plants are expensive, but the cost savings can be impressive. Changes in existing plants go into effect at the beginning of the next quarter.

Manufacturing Cost of Goods Sold

Four items comprise the total manufacturing cost: direct material, direct labor, overhead, and depreciation of the production facilities. In quarter 8, the material cost is $144,033 (line 1).

The figure for material comes from line 9 of the production analysis. The regular pay (line 2 on manufacturing cost of goods sold) for a production worker is $2,500. Fifty-three workers are available for the quarter plus the 3 people hired for a total of 56. No workers were laid off, so there are no costs associated with layoffs. The employees produced 1,000 units in overtime (line 4) for a total cost of $15,000 ($15 × 1,000). In quarter 8, you had available 53 workers, which made 17 whole three-person crews or a maximum of 17,000 units of regular production, but you assembled 18,000 units; thus you had 1,000 units overtime. The hiring cost of $9,000 reflects the 3 workers you hired (line 5) in quarter 8. The variable overhead (line 6) is currently applied at the rate of 50 percent of the total labor cost. The depreciation of $91,000 is derived by the straight line method. The production facilities have a five-year or twenty-quarter life with zero salvage value ($1,820,000 plant assets × 5 percent). Total manufacturing cost (line 8) is the sum of the material, labor, overhead, and depreciation, or $481,033 (for quarter 8).

The finished-goods inventory of $25,841 at the beginning of quarter 8 (line 9) is added to the total manufacturing cost (line 8) to obtain the total cost of goods (line 10) for quarter 8 of $506,874. At the conclusion of quarter 8, a physical inventory (line 11) is taken, and it reveals the existence of 3,189 units in the finished-goods inventory. Thus 15,554 units were sold (line 12) for $420,633, or a per unit cost of $27.04.

WAREHOUSING OPERATIONS

The warehousing operations statement gives the status of your finished-goods inventory in each of three areas. Presently in quarter 8 you have a warehouse in each area, including one attached to the assembly plant in Area 1. Warehouse expense is reflected as the $2 per unit cost of carrying inventory. Line 1 shows that in Areas 1, 2, and 3 you had 743, 0, and 0 units, respectively, in beginning inventory.

With production facilities currently located only in Area 1, you can see in line 2 that all 18,000 units were assembled in Area 1. Notice that this figure of 18,000 units agrees with the information in the statements of production analysis and manufacturing cost of goods sold. Line 3 shows the units available for sale before transfers.

Taking into consideration the expected sales in each area, you must now transfer finished goods into areas that have shortages. You are presently permitted to warehouse and transfer goods among Gidget's three areas for $4 per unit transferred. Looking at line 4 in the quarter 8 warehouse operations statement, you see that the decision was to transfer 6,000 units to Area 2 and 5,000 units to Area 3. The total cost for these transfers was $44,000, which is shown in line 10. The transfer price of $4 per unit will be subject to change in the future because of the demand on shippers, wage settlements among shippers, and other variables. If the transfer cost is prohibitive, you can reduce the cost by building additional plants in other areas. Later, if you have production facilities in other areas, you might transfer goods from Area 2 or 3. Line 6 gives the goods available for sale in each area after transfers.

The units sold by area, shown on line 7, reflect the sales effort and units available. Line 8 shows the inventory for the end of the quarter, which becomes your beginning inventory for the next quarter. In quarter 8, more units are available than demanded in Areas 2 and 3. When demand exceeds your supply, such as in Area 1, the units of sales lost are shown on line 9 as a positive figure. The excess units represent permanently lost sales, and these cause salespersons to become disgruntled. For each area in which you lose sales because of lack of supply, one salesperson resigns from the total sales force at the end of the quarter (see line 11 of selling and administrative expense analysis). If you have no salespersons in an area and still stock out, you will still lose a salesperson. The carry-over effect of some elements of the sales effort does not allow you to abandon a sales area except when the forecasted sales there are zero.

The cost of carrying inventory is determined by multiplying the current $2 carrying cost by the beginning inventory. The total cost of warehouse operations is the sum of the cost of units transferred plus the cost of carrying inventory. This figure is shown in line 12 of the warehouse operations statement and again in line 4 of the statement of income.

SELLING AND ADMINISTRATIVE EXPENSE ANALYSIS

The decisions reflected on the selling and administrative expense analysis statement determine your total sales effort exclusive of sales price, and, therefore, play a vital role in determining demand in each area. Remember that the simulation is dynamic and interactive. Active demand depends not only on your level of sales effort but on everyone else's sales efforts as well.

Sales Personnel

Sales personnel must be trained before they are ready to be a part of your sales effort. The training program (line 1) requires two quarters. For example, if you hire 1 salesperson in quarter 9, he or she will be in training in quarter 10 and ready to sell in quarter 11. The current cost of hiring the salesperson is $1,100 and the current salary is $3,500 per quarter for a total of $4,600 in quarter 10. Each salesperson is paid $3,500 while in training, and continues to make $3,500 per quarter after joining the trained sales force. As the simulation progresses, these salaries and hiring costs are subject to change.

In quarter 8, you have hired 1 salesperson (line 1) and have 2 in training (line 2), and you already have 10 trained, productive (regular) salespeople. These 10 people are assigned (line 3) to Areas 1, 2, and 3 in a 6-2-2 arrangement. The sales force is flexible and people can be transferred (unlike production workers) from area to area at your discretion. The total number in the sales force is the sum of the numbers hired, in training, and regular salespersons. In quarter 8, 13 are in sales at a cost of $46,600 for an average of $3,585 per salesperson for quarter 8.

The figure in line 11 of the selling and administrative expense analysis is the number of salespeople discharged and/or lost for the next quarter because your demand exceeds your supply (see line 9 of the warehouse operations statement) in any of the three areas. The maximum number of salespeople your team can lose due to stockouts is 3.

Advertising

National advertising is the advertising that affects all three areas simultaneously. It costs $3,000 per page and has an effect for three quarters. For example, the 11 pages of national advertising shown in line 5 in quarter 8 will benefit your sales effort to some extent in quarter 9 and less in quarter 10. Think of national advertising as ads placed in magazines such as *Time, Reader's Digest,* and so on. The effect of your national advertising depends on the industry level of advertising and is subject to diminishing marginal returns.

Local advertising at $900 per page costs less than national advertising but is effective for only one quarter and in the area designated. The advantage of advertising locally is concentration of effort. In quarter 8, the decision was to buy locally a total of 16 pages in a ratio by areas of 9-4-3 at a total cost of $14,400.

Product Improvements

Product improvements are changes in your product that make it more marketable. They might take the form of a change in technology or a change in packaging. Product improvements allow for product differentiation. Product improvements in quarter 8 cost $10,000 each, but the benefits are cumulative. Since you are limited to a maximum of three each quarter, the cumulative effects on market share can be impressive toward the end of the simulation.

Environment Information

To make good decisions, you need information about your present and future environment. Most companies obtain information about competitors' activities and the market and other relevant news. However, collecting relevant information requires research, which creates cost. If you have too little information during your decision making analysis, you increase your chances of making a poor decision. On the other hand, if you buy too much information, the cost of the extra information will be more than its value. For example, when making a price change it is best to know competitors' prices but knowledge of industry plant capacity may not be necessary. Figure 3.1 shows a form to help you evaluate your requests (the request to the computer is discussed in conjunction with Card 3 in Chapter 4). Note that the information requested and supplied in quarter 8 is for use in quarter 9. It is highly recommended that you buy environment information selectively each quarter. You will receive your market information when you receive your printouts each quarter.

Selling and Administrative Expenses

The administrative expenses of $25,000 shown in line 9 include executive salaries, office rent, and supplies. If plants are operated in two areas, administrative expenses are $35,000. In all three areas administrative expenses are $42,500. Changes in administrative expenses take place as plants are in construction and when a purchased plant begins to produce.

The total selling and administrative expense, then, is the sum of the costs of your sales effort, market information, and administration. This figure of $137,500 (line 10) is transferred to line 3 of the statement of income.

CASH FLOW

Accountants' income statements are prepared on an accrual basis in which revenues and expenses are matched for the current quarter. Since revenues and expenses do not necessarily represent cash flows, it is necessary to account separately for cash flow; the measurement of cash flow from all sources including operations provides valuable financial information. But, on the other hand, the measurement of cash flow is in no way a substitute for an income statement. It is conceivable that cash flow could be improving at the same time that income is deteriorating and vice versa.

Cash Receipts

Cash receipts represent all increases in cash during the quarter plus the cash balance brought forward from the previous quarter. The first item on your cash flow statement is the previous cash balance of $96,998 (line 1 of cash flow statement), designated as cash on hand at the beginning of the quarter.

The collection of accounts receivable (line 2) is the cash collections of your previous sales. You have no uncollectable accounts. The collection rate for the Gidget Company is 10 percent in the quarter sold, 50 percent in the next quarter, and 40 percent in the third quarter. Assume $500,000 in sales in quarter 9. The cash collection of the $500,000 will be $50,000 in quarter 9, $250,000 in quarter 10, and $200,000 in quarter 11. Similarly, cash collections in quarter 8 from accounts receivable represent 10 percent of sales in quarter 8, 50 percent of sales in quarter 7, and 40 percent of sales in quarter 6.

FIGURE 3.1

ENVIRONMENT INFORMATION FORM

Company ___Gidget Ind'y 1 Co.1___   Quarter ___8___

Circle column number of information desired and transfer cost to the last column.

				Cost of information	Cost to company	
67	Sales potential, in units, for four quarters in advance			$25,000		67

Quarter	Area 1	Area 2	Area 3

(68) Sales potential, in units, for one quarter only (one of the next four quarters)   Quarter _12_ $7,500   **$7,500** (68)
*   Area 1 _____ Area 2 _____ Area 3 _____

69   Number of salespersons in industry this quarter $2,000   69
Area 1 _____ Area 2 _____ Area 3 _____

70   Plant capacity, in product units, for industry this quarter $3,000   70

	Area 1	Area 2	Area 3
Present			
Under construction			
Ordered this quarter			

71   Number of pages of national advertising this quarter   Total _____ $1,500   71

72   Number of pages of local advertising this quarter $1,500   72
Area 1 _____ Area 2 _____ Area 3 _____

73   Sales, by company, this quarter $3,000   73

Co. #	Units	Co. #	Units	Co. #	Units
1		5		9	
2		6		10	
3		7		11	
4		8		12	

74   Sales price, by company, this quarter $2,000   74

Co. #	Price	Co. #	Price	Co. #	Price
1		5		9	
2		6		10	
3		7		11	
4		8		12	

(75) News bulletin ___Material prices will not change in quarters 9 and 10.___ $1,000   **$1,000** (75)

TOTAL cost of environment survey report   **$8,500**

* Administrator will furnish this information for quarter 8.

Line 3 represents the stock, bond, and plant sales income. Stock and bond issues will be received in the quarter in which they are requested. If you request a $700,000 bond issue in quarter 9, you will receive the cash at the beginning of quarter 9. In the case of plant sales, there is a delay of one quarter in receiving payment, so that if you sell a 5,000-unit plant for $350,000 in quarter 9 you will receive the cash at the beginning of quarter 10, and retain use of the plant during quarter 9.

If you have a short term investment withdrawal the cash will also appear in line 3.

The total cash available, shown in line 4, is the sum of the three items above and is the source of your cash with the exception of the short-term loan in line 18 (discussed in a later paragraph).

Cash Payments

Your cash payments are listed in lines 5 through 15. Line 5 shows your material purchases and is the sum of the material receipts plus the carrying cost ($1 times beginning inventory). You pay for the material when it is received, not when it is ordered. The $161,600 (line 5) represents the material received in quarter 8 (line 2 of production analysis) plus the carrying cost (line 8) or $160,000 plus $1,600.

The next item, the net short-term interest, represents the interest on your beginning short-term loan balance less any interest revenue you might have from a short-term investment. Net short-term interest would, of course, be negative if investment revenue exceeded loan interest. The short-term loan interest rate printed to the right of next quarter's interest payment is based on last quarter's debt to asset ratio. The short-term interest rate floats and is dependent on the rate set by the game administrator plus your debt to assets ratio as follows:

Debt/Assets Ratio	Adjustment
.00 to .05	−2
.05 to .10	−1.5
.10 to .15	−1.0
.15 to .20	−0.5
.20 to .30	0.0
.30 to .40	+0.5
.40 to .50	+1.0
.50 to .60	+1.5
Over .60	+2.0

The figure for interest on bonds payable in line 7 shows your quarterly interest on outstanding bonds. Interest starts the quarter after a bond is received and continues through the quarter of payoff. Also included in line 7 is the 3 percent prepayment penalty on bonds. For example, if you wish to pay $50,000 above the normal principal payment on bond 1, the prepayment penalty would be 3 percent of $50,000 or $1,500. Currently you have two bonds outstanding each with an interest rate of 9 percent. Bonds are discussed more during the discussion of the statements of financial position at the end of this chapter.

The declared dividends paid in line 8 and the income tax paid in line 9 are calculated in the statement of income for quarter 7 and paid in cash in quarter 8. If dividends and stock retirement occur in the same quarter, then the stock is retired prior to the payment of the dividends. If income tax paid is negative because of an overpayment previously, then you have a credit in your income tax account.

The bond and stock retirement in line 10 represents the normal principal retirement of outstanding bonds plus any payment you make in addition to the normal payments. If you decide to retire a portion of your outstanding stock, the retirement will also be reflected in the bond and stock retirement account. (These will be discussed in Chapter 4.)

Down payments and regular payments on any plants you decide to build are shown in line 11. If you buy a plant already built, the payment for it will also be reflected in this account.

The short-term loan plus the investment payments figure in line 12 represents the repayment of your short-term loans. For example, if you request a short-term loan of $100,000 in quarter 9, the normal repayment schedule will be $50,000 in quarter 10 and $50,000 in quarter 11. (Accelerated repayment is discussed in Chapter 4.) The short-term repayment of $107,172 shown in line 12 is due to short-term loans made in quarters 6 and 7.

Labor plus variable overhead in line 13 is the sum of the cost of production labor plus the overhead from the statement of manufacturing cost of goods sold. The figure of $246,000 comes from $164,000 shown in line 5 of the manufacturing cost of goods sold plus the $82,000 in overhead shown in line 6.

The warehouse and inventory carrying cost of $45,486 in line 14 is the sum of the cost of transferring finished goods and the carrying of inventory from line 12 of your warehouse operation statement.

The selling and administrative expense of $137,500 shown in line 15 is the total sum from line 10 of your selling and administrative expense analysis statement.

Cash Balance and Needed Borrowing

You obtain the net cash balance of a $91,340 deficit in line 17 by subtracting total cash payments, line 16, from the total cash available, shown in line 4. The net cash balance represents your cash situation before any short-term loans.

The short-term loan amount shown in line 18 represents either your requesting or the computer's granting you a short-term loan because of your deficit cash position. Using your quarter 8 print-out as an example, you see that the net cash balance was a deficit of $91,340. A short-term loan of $150,000 was requested. Therefore, as shown in line 19, you have a cash balance of $58,660. The interest rate for short-term loans is currently 10 percent per annum or 2 1/2 percent per quarter. Do not forget that the interest rate floats as it depends on your debt to assets ratio. On the other hand, if you had not requested a short-term loan, the computer would have loaned you exactly $91,340 at an interest rate of up to 30 percent per annum. The higher the ratio is, the higher the interest will be. If, in the same example, a short-term loan had been requested for $90,000, which would not have been enough, the computer would have ignored your request and loaned you $91,340 at the higher interest rate, the increment of which would then be reflected in line 20. Of course, you want your company under no circumstances to receive a computer loan.

Forecasting Cash Flows

The cash flow statement, like most of the other statements, helps you forecast an estimate of your next quarter's cash flow. It should be emphasized that the forecasts are only estimates because the computer has no idea of your next quarter's plans. For example, the forecast of your accounts receivable for next quarter is $541,128, but this figure will increase by 10 percent of your sales revenue in the next quarter. Similarly, from line 11, the forecast for payments of plant next quarter is zero, but if you make the decision to order a plant in quarter 9, then the down payment will be added and will be reflected in the next quarter's cash flow. The forecasts that are correct because they are calculated automatically are lines 5, 6, 7, 8, and 9. Line 10 is correct unless you elect to accelerate payment on bond 1.

Make special note of the question marks that appear in lines 13, 14, and 15. In these cases the computer has no idea what your plans are and therefore is not willing to make a forecast. Line 16 is the sum of the forecasted payments with the exception of lines 13, 14, and 15.

FINANCIAL STATEMENTS

Statement of Income

The statement of income reflects this quarter's operations plus a year-to-date summary. The statement is based on absorption costing, which simply means that fixed manufacturing overhead, depreciation in your case, is assigned to the units produced as a product cost. Income tax is computed on the quarterly earnings at the rate of 50 percent of line 8. If there is a loss in the quarter, taxes will be zero for the quarter, excluding the fourth quarter of the calendar year. In the fourth quarter, taxes are adjusted such that your cumulative income for the year is taxed at 50 percent. There are two special exceptions to this rule.

The first is the loss carry back. If cumulative earnings for the year are negative, and if taxes were paid in the previous year, then taxes are refunded up to half of your loss.

Year	Income	Taxes Paid	Refund
1	$100,000	$50,000	$0
2	−$20,000	$0	$10,000
or			
1	$10,000	$5,000	$0
2	−$40,000	$0	$5,000

In quarter 8, cumulative earnings for the year are −$39,692. According to line 9 in the statement of income for quarter 7, $32,758 in taxes had been paid this calendar year. Therefore, in quarter 8 these taxes are refunded. Also, up to half of the cumulative loss for the year, or taxes paid in the previous calendar year, whichever figure is least, is refunded. In quarter 4, line 9 of the statement of income indicates $27,116 in taxes paid; therefore, $19,845 is refunded from the previous year. Total refund equals $19,845 plus $32,758 or $52,603, rounded to $52,604 on line 9 of the statement of income for quarter 8.

The second is the loss carry forward. If cumulative earnings for the year are positive and the previous year's earnings are negative, then the previous year's loss can be carried forward to the current year's earnings.

Year	Income	Taxes
1	−$20,000	$0
2	$100,000	$40,000

In either case, you may not carry losses forward or back more than one calendar year,.

Dividends declared are deducted from net income after taxes, and the net is added to retained earnings in stockholders' equity. Items 14 and 15 are per share earnings and dividends.

Statement of Financial Position

The statement of financial position represents the financial condition of your company on the last day of the quarter. It consists of a listing of the assets and liabilities of your company and the stockholders' equity or investment. A few items warrant special discussion.

Notes payable in line 11 reflects your short-term loans, and in addition, your outstanding payment on any plants.

Bonds payable in line 15 shows the balance in each of your two outstanding bond accounts. Each team is allowed only two bonds at any given time. Before a team obtains a third bond, it must retire its first bond. If the bond is not retired, the computer will reject the new request. Of course, if you have only one bond outstanding, you merely request the second issue.

The stock market price of stock in line 22 is calculated by using the following variables in different proportions: previous stock price, earnings per share, losses per share, continuous quarters of profit or loss, amount of dividend, number of continuous quarters a dividend has been paid, and the price-to-earnings ratio.

SUMMARY

Up to now, you have read about the general background of the simulation, the details of the decisions you are to make, and the feedback you will receive from them. The next chapter describes the method you will use to record your decisions in preparation for having them processed by the administrator. The decision sheet, an intermediate step before the cards are punched for the computer, helps you relate all your decisions by seeing them on one form.

4

The Decision Sheet

This chapter describes the manner in which you should record your decisions. The decision sheet used for quarter 8 is reproduced in Figure 4.1. After Appendix B, ten copies of the decision sheet are included for recording your future decisions.

Looking at the decision sheet in Figure 4.1, you observe that across the top of the sheet there are 80 columns corresponding to the 80 columns of a computer card. Looking down the sheet, you notice 6 rows of input data; thus each decision sheet will consist of 6 computer-data cards. The game administrator will inform you of the method of submitting your decision.

To complete the decision sheet, it is imperative that you insert input data in the correct columns. (Computer corrections and the cost of errors are presented in the list of error messages in Appendix A.) In all cases, all input data are right justified—that is, placed to the right—and no decimal points are allowed. For example, in Card 1 the number of pages of national advertising is entered in columns 1 through 6. Be sure that the last digit of the number is entered in column 6. In quarter 8, 11 pages of national advertising were requested; therefore, the number "11" is keypunched in columns 5 and 6 of Card 1. If you make an error and put the number in column 4 instead of column 5, you will record a request of 110 pages of national advertising. At $3,000 per page, this comes to $330,000—an expensive investment to say the least! The moral is: make no mistakes. Check and double-check should be your standard operating procedure.

Cards 1 through 6 illustrate each of the decision cards item by item.

FIGURE 4.1

DECISION SHEET for TEMPOMATIC IV (DO NOT PUNCH DECIMAL POINTS; PLACE LAST DIGIT OF EACH DECISION IN RIGHT COLUMN OF BOX)

CARD 1

| 1|2|3|4|5|6|7|8|9|10|11|12|13|14|15|16|17|18|19|20|21|22|23|24|25|26|27|28|29|30|31|32|33|34|35|36|37|38|39|40|41|42|43|44|45|46|47|48|49|50|51|52|53|54|55|56|57|58|59|60|61|62|63|64|65|66|67|68|69|70|71|72|73|74|75|76|77|78|79|80 |

Natl. Adv. No. Pgs.: `11` — `9` `4` `3` `6` `2` `1` `2` — `40` `1` `GIDGET` `22` `51`

| Area 1 | Area 2 | Area 3 | | No. of Prod. Improvement | Area 1 | Area 2 | Area 3 | Company Name | Ind'y Number | Company Number + 50 |

Local Advertising–Number Pgs. | Number of Salespersons | Sales Price Per Unit

CARD 2

| 1|2|3|4|5|6|7|8|9|10|11|12|13|14|15|16|17|18|19|20|21|22|23|24|25|26|27|28|29|30|31|32|33|34|35|36|37|38|39|40|41|42|43|44|45|46|47|48|49|50|51|52|53|54|55|56|57|58|59|60|61|62|63|64|65|66|67|68|69|70|71|72|73|74|75|76|77|78|79|80 |

`8` `1` — `6000` `5000` `11000` `11000` `11000` `GIDGET` `102`

| Quarter | Number of Salespersons Hired | Number of Salespersons Discharged | Area 1 | Area 2 | Area 3 | Total Trfd. | Area 1 | Area 2 | Area 3 | Company Name | Co. No. |

Units Transferred To | Units Transferred From

CARD 3

| 1|2|3|4|5|6|7|8|9|10|11|12|13|14|15|16|17|18|19|20|21|22|23|24|25|26|27|28|29|30|31|32|33|34|35|36|37|38|39|40|41|42|43|44|45|46|47|48|49|50|51|52|53|54|55|56|57|58|59|60|61|62|63|64|65|66|67|68|69|70|71|72|73|74|75|76|77|78|79|80 |

`200000` — `150000` `8500` `4` `1` `103`

| Area 1 | Area 2 | Area 3 | Short-Term Loan Requested–$ | Total S-T Loan Repayment–$ | % of Profit to Dividend | Dividend Per Share–¢ | Cost of Environment Information | A|B|C|D|E|F|G|H| Environment Information | Co. No. |

Material Ordered–Units | Plant Ordered Constructed–Units

CARD 4

| 1|2|3|4|5|6|7|8|9|10|11|12|13|14|15|16|17|18|19|20|21|22|23|24|25|26|27|28|29|30|31|32|33|34|35|36|37|38|39|40|41|42|43|44|45|46|47|48|49|50|51|52|53|54|55|56|57|58|59|60|61|62|63|64|65|66|67|68|69|70|71|72|73|74|75|76|77|78|79|80 |

`18000` `3` `104`

| Area 1 | Area 2 | Area 3 | Production Workers Hired–Number | Production Workers Discharged–Number | Deposit–$ | Withdraw–$ | A1 | A2 | A3 | Cost | Co. No. |

Total Actual Production–Units | Short-Term Investment | Worker Layoffs

CARD 5

| 1|2|3|4|5|6|7|8|9|10|11|12|13|14|15|16|17|18|19|20|21|22|23|24|25|26|27|28|29|30|31|32|33|34|35|36|37|38|39|40|41|42|43|44|45|46|47|48|49|50|51|52|53|54|55|56|57|58|59|60|61|62|63|64|65|66|67|68|69|70|71|72|73|74|75|76|77|78|79|80 |

| Number | Price | Number | Amount $ | Interest–% per yr. × 100 | Amount of 1st Payment | Qtr. of 1st Pay. | Freq. of Pay. | Amount of Other Payment | Extra Payment 1st Bond | Per Crew | Crew Size | Salary $/per | Hiring $/per | Co. No. `105` |

Stock Issue–Share/¢ | Stock Retired–Share/¢ | Bonds: Issuance and Payment | Productivity | Salesperson

CARD 6

| 1|2|3|4|5|6|7|8|9|10|11|12|13|14|15|16|17|18|19|20|21|22|23|24|25|26|27|28|29|30|31|32|33|34|35|36|37|38|39|40|41|42|43|44|45|46|47|48|49|50|51|52|53|54|55|56|57|58|59|60|61|62|63|64|65|66|67|68|69|70|71|72|73|74|75|76|77|78|79|80 |

| Reg. Pay $/Qtr. | Overtime ¢/Unit | Hiring Cost $/Person | High Price | Med. Price | Low Price | Sale Price $ | Accumulated Depreciation | Area | Capacity–Units | Purchase Price $ | Area | Capacity–Units | Option `106` Co. No. |

Prod. Worker Pay: Change to ($) | Material Cost: Change to ($) | Sale of Plant | Purchase of Plant

CARD 1 *Advertising, Salespersons, Product Improvement, and Sales Price*

It was pointed out earlier, in the selling and administrative expense analysis, that national advertising costs $3,000 per page, and it benefits the Gidget Company for three quarters. The 11 pages bought in quarter 8 will benefit sales in quarter 8, in quarter 9 and, to a lesser extent, in quarter 10. All three areas, however, receive equal benefit.

Local advertising costs $900 per page but benefits the company for only one quarter. The 9 pages bought in Area 1 will benefit the sales effort in quarter 8 and in Area 1 only. Local advertising is effective only in the area advertised.

The number of regular salespersons recorded (see the selling and administrative expense analysis, line 3) represents the allocation of the salespersons in the three areas. The more salespersons you have in an area, the greater the sales effort will be in that area. In quarter 8 you have assigned 6 salespersons to Area 1, 2 to Area 2, and 2 to Area 3. This is your distribution of the 10 salespersons available. Note that in quarter 9, you will have 11 salespersons to assign (line 3).

Product improvements, you recall, make your product more marketable because of such things as changes in technology, quality, and style, but you are limited to three product improvements per quarter at a cost of $10,000 per improvement. The effects are cumulative; that is, the computer keeps account of how many product improvements you have made in the past.

The decision as to sales price should be made in conjunction with the other input decisions on Card 1, but it is restricted currently to the range of $34 minimum and $47 maximum per TEMPOMATIC. Prices may be changed by more than one dollar but must be always in whole dollars. For example, the price can be changed from $40 to $43. Sales results are affected by your sales price relative to that of the other teams and by your current sales price relative to your previous sales price. To maintain your market share you need corresponding changes in the mix of advertising, salespersons, and product improvements as your sales price changes. In other words, there is an elastic demand.

The game administrator will instruct you when you are to use Area 2 and 3 fields.

Your company's name should be placed in columns 55-60. This is the only time you may use alphabetic characters. The game administrator will assign (or let you assign) a company name for your team at the beginning of the simulation.

Insert industry number.

Each team will be assigned a sort code number. Assume, for example, that your company is company 1. In Card 1, columns 79 and 80, you will insert that number plus 50, in this case 51. This sort code assists in assembling the data check for computation.

CARD 1

Field	Value	Columns
Nat. Adv. No. Pgs.	11	1
Local Advertising–Number Pgs. — Area 1	9	
Local Advertising–Number Pgs. — Area 2	4	
Local Advertising–Number Pgs. — Area 3	3	
Number of Salespersons — Area 1	6	
Number of Salespersons — Area 2	2	
Number of Salespersons — Area 3	2	
No. of Prod. Improvement	1	
Sales Price Per Unit — Area 1	40	
Sales Price Per Unit — Area 2		
Sales Price Per Unit — Area 3		
Company Name	GIDGET	55-60
Ind'y Number	22	
Company Number + 50	51	79-80

CARD 2 *Salespersons and Product Transfer*

The first item to be entered on Card 2 is the quarter; since we are dealing with quarter 8, this is the number to be inserted in column 6.

The number of salespersons entered on Card 2 (see line 1 of the selling and administrative expense analysis) represents the number of salespersons you wish to hire. The salespersons hired in quarter 8 will be in training in quarter 9 and producing in quarter 10.

The salesperson discharged figure represents the number of salespersons you feel you no longer need. The number of salespersons you discharge is in addition to the number you lose when sales demand exceeds your supply of finished goods in each of the areas. Discharged salespersons leave at the end of the quarter and are shown on line 11.

The units-transferred-to field indicates the finished goods to be transferred from one warehouse area to another. In quarter 8, the decision was to transfer 6,000 units to Area 2 and 5,000 to Area 3. The total number of units is entered in the next field.

The units-transferred-from field of this card represents the source warehouse in which the units were originally located. In quarter 8, all 11,000 units were transferred from Area 1.

The company name is inserted on Card 2 as it was on Card 1.

As in Card 1, you should enter a card sort number. Retaining the previous example number 1, you should insert 1 in column 78. In addition, you must enter a 0 in column 79 and a 2 in column 80 (indicating Card 2) to complete the sort code.

CARD 2

Card fields:
- Quarter (col 6): 8
- Number of Salespersons Hired: 1
- Number of Salespersons Discharged
- Units Transferred To — Area 1; Area 2: 6000; Area 3: 5000; Total Trfd.: 11000
- Units Transferred From — Area 1: 11000; Area 2; Area 3
- Company Name: GIDGET
- Co. No. (cols 78–80): 1 0 2

CARD 3 *Material and Plant Orders, Loans, Dividends,*
and Market Information

The first item on Card 3 is the number of units in your material orders, reported in line 6 of the production analysis. Since material must be ordered one quarter in advance, the material ordered in quarter 8 will not be received until quarter 9. In quarter 8, 20,000 units of material were ordered for Area 1. No material was ordered for Area 2 or Area 3.

The plants-ordered field of Card 3 represents in units the plants you wish to build. If you wanted to build a 5,000-unit plant in Area 2, you would enter 5,000 in columns 27-30. (Do not confuse the recording of building a plant with that of purchasing a plant. If you wish to buy a plant, the decision is entered on Card 6 only. If you filled in both places, you would build a 5,000-unit plant and buy a 5,000-unit plant in Area 2, for a total of 10,000 units in that area.)

The short-term loan reported on line 18 of the cash flow statement is entered next on Card 3. The $150,000 requested in quarter 8 will be paid back automatically in two payments of $75,000, in quarters 9 and 10.

The total short-term repayment field in this card is provided so that you may increase but not decrease your short-term repayments. For example, in quarter 9, you are scheduled to repay $75,000, shown in line 12 of the cash flow statement. If you wish to pay $100,000 to avoid the interest charges, you may insert 100000.

You can declare dividends in one of two ways, as was discussed in Chapter 3 under Income Statement. Be sure you have enough retained earnings to cover the dividends. When you want to pay:
1. a certain percentage of your after-tax in dividends, you use columns 53 and 54. If, for example, you want to pay 10 percent, put 1 in column 53 and 0 in column 54. OR (use only one method)
2. a certain amount per share, you use columns 55 to 60. For example, if you want to pay a $.25 dividend per share, put 2 in column 59 and 5 in column 60.
Note the minimum dividend that will improve your stock price is $.05.

Marketing information is requested in two parts.

1. The cost (8500) is obtained from the Environment Information form (see its discussion in Chapter 3). Be sure to enter enough to pay for information requested—too little will result in no information. The game administrator will also use this field to add additional charges such as fines or make cash payments back to you.
2. Automatic processing of information requires the use of columns 67-75.
   Leave blank for no information; enter 1 for information in a category. Sales potential (column 68) can be requested from 1 to 4 quarters ahead—enter the number. (Note that the 4 entered in quarter 8 asks for quarter 12 potential.)

   Sales potential, 4 quarters ahead
   Sales potential, 1 quarter, number of quarters ahead.
   Number of salespersons, industry
   Plant capacity, industry
   Number pages national advertising
   Number pages local advertising
   Sales by company, this quarter
   Sales price by company, this quarter
   News bulletin.

Enter the card sort number as in Card 2.

CARD 3

Material Ordered—Units: Area 1 (2 0 0 0 0), Area 2, Area 3
Plant Ordered Constructed—Units: Area 1, Area 2, Area 3
Short-Term Loan Requested-$ (1 5 0 0 0 0)
Total S-T Loan Repayment-$
% of Profit to Dividend
Dividend Per Share-¢
Cost of Environment Information (8 5 0 0)
A B C D E F G H I Environment Information (4 ... 1)
Co. No. (1 0 3)

CARD 4 *Production and Investment*

CARD 4

Total Actual Production—Units

Area 1	Area 2	Area 3
1 8 0 0		

The total actual production, reported as units assembled in line 2 of the warehouse operations report, represents the total amount of production, regular plus overtime, that you desire per area. Maximum regular production is limited by plant capacity, the number of crews working regular hours, and the quantity of raw material on hand (see line 18 on production analysis). Twenty percent of regular hours can be added for overtime. Eighteen thousand units of total actual production were desired in quarter 8 in Area 1. Therefore, 18,000 is entered for Area 1.

Production Workers Hired—Number

Area 1	Area 2	Area 3
3		

The figure for production workers hired, reported in line 16 of the production analysis, represents the number of workers hired in each area. In quarter 8, 3 workers were hired in Area 1. Production workers require one quarter for training; be sure to allow for them one quarter in advance of when you will need them.

Production Workers Discharged—Number

Area 1	Area 2	Area 3

Enter here the number of production workers you wish to discharge at the beginning of the quarter. Line 11 of the production analysis in quarter 8 shows the number discharged as zero. The number lost due to turnover (2 in Area 1) is not included here as it is calculated automatically.

Short-Term Investment

Deposit-$	Withdraw-$

Excess cash can be invested (reported in line 3 of the statement of financial position) to earn a rate of interest set by the game administrator. If you wish to make a short-term investment, enter the amount here. Interest income will reduce your net interest expense account, reported in line 7 of the statement of income in the quarter following the investment.

Enter here dollar withdrawals you wish to make from short-term investments. The computer will make withdrawals on request only and will reimburse you after one quarter; e.g., a quarter 9 request for cash reimbursement is granted in quarter 10. This is reported in line 3 of the cash flow statement. Thus, if you wish to invest money for one quarter, the entry to deposit and withdraw must be made at the same time.

Worker Layoffs

A1	A2	A3	Cost

Enter the number of workers laid off for each area and the layoff cost per worker. Remember that laid off workers automatically return the following quarter.

Co. No.

1 0 4	

Enter the card sort number as in Card 2.

CARD 5 *Stocks and Bonds*

This card is used to obtain money for expansion and fixed investments and to reduce equity and fixed liabilities. Entries in this card require approval of game administrator. Figures shown are for illustrative purposes. For most quarters, this card will be blank except for the sort code.)

Issuance of stock increases the equity position of your company. The example here specifies the issuance of 5,000 shares of stock at $11 (entered as 1100 cents) per share. This value can never be less than par value. The sum of $55,000 will be received in the quarter requested, the cash receipt reported in line 3 in the cash flow statement of income, common stock increased by $50,000 (5,000 × $10 or par value) in line 17 in the statement of financial position, and accumulated retained earnings in line 18 increased by $5,000 ($55,000 − $50,000). Note that you may not issue stock below par, which is $10.00 and will not be changing for the duration of the game.

Retirement of stock reduces the equity position of your company. For example, 3,000 shares might be retired at a price of $13 (entered as 1300). The retirement will be reflected as a cash payment in the cash flow statement, line 10, and the number of shares of stock outstanding will be reduced by 3,000 in the statement of income, line 15. Also, on the statement of financial position, the common stock (line 17) will be reduced by $30,000 and accumulated retained earnings (line 18) will be reduced by $9,000. Under no circumstances can stock retirements reduce retained earnings below zero.

The issuance of additional bonds is accomplished as in the following example. The entries show a request for an $800,000 loan at an agreed interest rate of 12.5 percent (entered as 1250) with a first payment of $50,000 in quarter 11 and $40,000 payments each quarter after that. As you can see, you have flexibility in the size of the loan, interest rate, and repayment schedule. The values must be approved by the game administrator. Cash received is received at the beginning of the quarter requested and is reported in line 3 on the cash flow statement, and the bond payable is reported in line 15 in the statement of financial position.

Note the two bonds in line 15 in the statement of financial position in quarter 8. If you were to request $800,000 as in the example above, you would need to retire the first bond, as you have a maximum of two bonds outstanding. To do this you enter $160,000 here ($200,000 in bond payable less $40,000 agreed payment next quarter). The computer will charge you 3 percent of the $160,000 as added bond interest for all early retirements of bonds and will move the second bond into the zeroed first bond's position. No bond requests will be processed when a second bond exists without first paying off the first bond.

The game administrator may offer you an opportunity to enter a new production worker productivity per crew and/or a new production worker crew size. For example, you may be allowed to change productivity to 1200 and the crew size to two. Using the example of productivity being changed to 1200 in quarter 8 the worker productivity without overtime would be 26 crews (53 divided by 2) times 1200 or 67,200 units. Productivity and crew size change goes into effect the quarter the change is made.

Periodically, it may be appropriate to change salespersons' salaries and/or hiring cost. For example, if the salary is changed to $4,000 and hiring cost to $1,000, then this would be entered as 4000 and 1000, respectively. These changes go into effect the quarter the change is made.

Enter the card sort number as in Card 2.

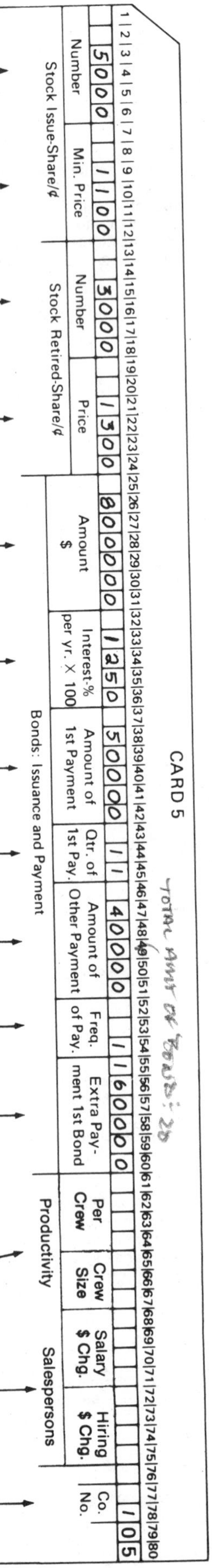

CARD 5

Stock Issue-Share/¢	Number	5000
Stock Issue-Share/¢	Min. Price	1100
Stock Retired-Share/¢	Number	3000
Stock Retired-Share/¢	Price	1300
Bonds: Issuance and Payment	Amount $	800000
Bonds: Issuance and Payment	Interest % per yr. × 100	1250
Bonds: Issuance and Payment	Amount of 1st Payment	50000
Bonds: Issuance and Payment	Qtr. of 1st Pay.	11
Bonds: Issuance and Payment	Amount of Other Payment	40000
Bonds: Issuance and Payment	Freq. ment of Pay.	1
Bonds: Issuance and Payment	Extra Payment 1st Bond	160000
Productivity	Per Crew	
Productivity	Crew Size	
Salespersons	Salary $ Chg.	
Salespersons	Hiring $ Chg.	
Co. No.		105

(handwritten: TOTAL AMT OF BONDS: 2D)

CARD 6 *Labor and Material Costs and Plant Transactions*
(figures shown are for illustrative purposes)

Inflation or contract negotiations may require increased worker costs. These changes are made as in the hypothetical example shown. If you insert the figures shown, regular pay would be changed to $2,650 per quarter, overtime to $16 (enter as 1600) per unit, and hiring cost to $3,600 per new employee. These three sections will be left blank except when administrator directs otherwise.

These three sections are to make changes in prices of material; otherwise they are blank. The vendors (again administrator) may increase prices. For hypothetical example, a price rise of $1 is ordered. You would add $1 to the current price (10, 9, 8) and enter as shown in the example.

When selling a plant, determine size and obtain accumulated depreciation from game administrator. Subtract accumulated depreciation from original cost to obtain a basis for negotiating a sales price with administrator. Enter values as explained in example. Suppose you plan to sell 5,000 units of original plant (Area 1) in quarter 8; the cost is $500,000 (5,000×$100), the accumulated depreciation is $225,000, and the negotiated sales price is $200,000. You enter the figures as shown. You have incurred a book loss of $75,000 (sales price less (cost less accumulated depreciation)). You have the use of the plant in quarter 8. In quarter 9, your plant capacity is reduced 5,000 units, you receive $200,000 of cash (line 3, cash flow statement) and lines 7, 8, and 18 of financial position statement are adjusted by $500,000, $225,000 and $750,000 respectively. If the game administrator negotiates a price with no book loss or gain, leave the accumulated depreciation field blank.

When you purchase a plant, you must negotiate a price with game administrator (usually higher than construction cost). Suppose you buy a 5000 unit plant in Area 2 for $600,000 in quarter 8; you make entries in fields as shown. In quarter 9, you can use the capacity. Entries will be made in line 19 of production analysis, line 11 of cash flow statement, and line 7 of statement of financial position. The cost of technological improvements must be entered under purchase price; no entries are required for area and capacity. Note: if technological improvements are made simultaneously with a plant purchase, enter the total expense under purchase price.

Technological improvements can be made to existing plant facilities by entering an option number corresponding to a set of alternatives provided by the game administrator. The game administrator will inform you of the possibility. Note, however, that technological improvements go into effect the quarter they are entered. Game administrator will provide details.

The last item on the decision sheet to be completed is the sort code, 106 in this case.

CARD 6

Prod. Worker Pay: Change to ($)	Reg. Pay $/Qtr.	2650
	Overtime ¢/Unit	1600
	Hiring Cost $/Person	3600
Material Cost: Change to ($)	High Price	11
	Med. Price	10
	Low Price	9
Sale of Plant	Sale Price $	200000
	Accumulated Depreciation	225000
	Area	1
	Capacity-Units	5000
Purchase of Plant	Purchase Price $	600000
	Area	2
	Capacity-Units	5000
	Opt. No.	
	Co. No.	106

Making Your Decisions

If you have never played Tempomatic IV before, you should study the first four chapters carefully, especially Chapters 3 and 4. Your understanding of the operating statements and decision sheet will directly affect your company's income. Next you should study the past performance of your company, as shown in the operating statements in the Appendix, in order to gain insight into what kinds of decisions have been made in the past and what must be done in the future to insure Gidget's prosperity. Only then will you be ready to make your first decision.

DECISION SHEET CHECK LIST

Following are a number of questions that your management team should raise and answer. The decisions that result from them and that you subsequently record on your decision sheet will govern your success. For example, questions 1 through 5 below determine your company's total sales effort and thus your share of the product demand.

1. How much national advertising do you need?
2. How much local advertising do you need and in what areas?
3. How should you assign the available salespersons?
4. What product improvements are needed?
5. What will be the Tempomatic selling price?
6. Are additional salespersons needed to increase sales effort?
7. Should any salespersons be discharged?
8. What quantity of finished goods is to be transferred to what areas?
9. From which areas are the finished goods to be transferred?
10. How much raw material will you order for each area?
11. How much total actual production (including regular production and overtime) is needed in the three areas?
12. Are any additional production workers needed because of turnover or increased capacity?
13. Are any workers to be laid off because of a reduction in production? (The cost decision must be approved by the game administrator.)
14. Are any additional or new plants needed?
15. Is the cash position such that you should make a short-term investment?
16. Is the cash position such that you must withdraw cash from the short-term investment to cover the next quarter's cash deficit?
17. Is a short-term loan needed to insure that the cash flow does not end in a deficit position?
18. Is there any excess cash that can be used to increase the short-term repayment?
19. How is capital expansion to be financed, by stocks or bonds?
20. If financed by bonds, how much and what terms? Are there two bond issues?

21. If financed by stock, how much and at what price?
22. Should some stock be retired? If so, how much and at what price?
23. How much payment, in addition to the normal repayment of the first bond, should you make?
24. Will you change production workers' costs?
25. Will you change material prices?
26. Is it necessary to sell an existing plant due to shifts in long-run demands?
27. Is it necessary to buy an existing plant due to shifts in demands?
28. What environment information will help the company management make better decisions in the future?
29. Are there any dividends to be paid? If so, what percent of profits or cents per share should they represent?

SUMMARY SHEET

The rest of this chapter is devoted to a presentation in tabular form of the data discussed in the rest of the text. You will need this information for your first decision making. In subsequent decisions, some of the values will change, reflecting changing conditions as well as changes in the actions of the game administrator and, most important, in your own actions.

The following data are a summary of the information for Tempomatic IV at the start of quarter 9.

Product price per kit	
Present	$40
Minimum price change	$1
Price range	$34–47
Sales Promotion	
Salespersons (each)	
Salary per quarter	$3,500
Hiring cost	$4,600
Quarters in training	2
Advertising cost per page	
National	$3,000
Local	$900
Product improvement cost (each)	$10,000
Product area transfer price per kit moved	$4
Production and purchasing	
Material purchase cost per kit per order per area	
1–10,000	$10
10,000–19,999	$9
20,000 +	$8
Advance quarters required for receipt of kits ordered	1
Percent probability of 80% receipt per order	7
Kit quantity per Tempomatic	1
Beginning inventory carrying charges per kit per quarter	
Raw material	$1
Finished product	$2
Plant	
Minimum new purchase size in kit capacity	5,000
Additions in kit capacity	1,000

Plant cost per kit (units)	$100
Construction time in quarters	2
Percent depreciation per quarter	5
Production personnel	
Workers per crew	3
Kit production per crew per quarter	1,000
Hiring cost per worker	$3,000
Quarters in training	1
Regular wage per worker	$2,500
Overtime pay per kit	$15
Maximum overtime as percent of production	20
Production workers per interval when turnover occurs	20
Production workers lost per interval by area	1
Percent probability of additional worker loss	
One worker	7
A second worker	3
Layoff cost	administrator
Crew size change	
Productivity change	

Finance	
Percent of sales income received in cash each quarter	
Quarter of sale	10
First quarter after sale	50
Second quarter after sale	40
Plant payment as percent of cost	
Down	20
Balance in construction	80
Short-term loans	
Percent interest on opening quarterly balance—annual rate	10
Maximum allowable ratio ratio equity to debt	80
Short-term investment percent interest on opening quarterly balance—annual rate	5
Charge for extra bond payment—percent of payment	3

Costing	
Variable overhead as percent of total labor cost	50
Information (See Figure 3.1)	Variable
Administration expenses per quarter—plant in one area	$25,000
plants in two areas	$35,000
plants in three areas	$42,500
Income tax as percentage of net income	50
Dividends on net income after taxes are percent of net income or cents per share.	

Average Forecast per Company

Quarter	Area 1	Area 2	Area 3
1	6,200	4,200	2,300
2	6,100	4,100	2,200
3	6,400	4,400	2,400
4	6,800	4,700	3,100
5	7,100	4,900	3,300
6	6,700	5,200	4,000
7	7,000	5,100	4,300
8	7,500	5,600	5,000

Appendix A
Error Messages

These are the messages that tell you when you have made a gross keypunch error or a grossly illogical decision. The computer is programmed to test for the figure that you punch. If it is larger or smaller than that of the statement, the computer will adjust to the figure indicated in the message. The figures in these messages are not meant to represent the range of values that you should consider but instead are limits that protect the company and the industry from costly mistakes. Each time the computer makes an adjustment, you are charged $2,000, which is added to your environment information expense. Each message is keyed to a number, which precedes it:

1. Number of national advertising pages requested exceeds 50. Request adjusted to 30.
2. Number of local advertising pages in Area 1 requested exceeds 50. Request adjusted to 20.
3. Number of local advertising pages in Area 2 requested exceeds 50. Request adjusted to 20.
4. Number of local advertising pages in Area 3 requested exceeds 50. Request adjusted to 20.
5. Number of salespersons assigned to Area 1 exceeds total salespersons available. Request adjusted to 0.
6. Number of salespersons assigned to Area 2 exceeds total salespersons available. Request adjusted to 0.
7. Number of salespersons assigned to Area 3 exceeds total salespersons available. Request adjusted to 0.
8. Product improvements requested exceed 3. Request adjusted to 3.
9. Sales price requested exceeds $47. Request adjusted to $47.
10. Sales price less than $34. Request adjusted to $34.
11. Salespersons hired exceed 9. Request adjusted to 9.
12. Salespersons discharged exceed 9. Request adjusted to 9.
13. Transfers to and from not equal. Adjustment made.
14. Goods transferred from Area 1 exceed goods available for transfer. Amount requested adjusted to maximum available for transfer. Adjustments are made in the goods transferred to an area if necessary.
15. Goods transferred from Area 2 exceed goods available for transfer. Amount requested adjusted to maximum available for transfer. Adjustments are made in the goods transferred to an area if necessary.
16. Goods transferred from Area 3 exceed goods available for transfer. Amount requested adjusted to maximum available for transfer. Adjustments are made in the goods transferred to an area if necessary.
17. Material ordered for Area 1 exceeds quantity equal to four times production and construction capacity in Area 1. Corrected to four times production and construction capacity.
18. Material ordered for Area 2 exceeds quantity equal to four times production and construction capacity in Area 2. Corrected to four times production and construction capacity.

19. Material ordered for Area 3 exceeds quantity equal to four times production and construction capacity in Area 3. Corrected to four times production and construction capacity.
20. Program assumes you meant to order a 5,000-unit plant when you inserted 1 in columns 24, 30, or 36.
21. Program assumes you meant to order a 10,000-unit plant when you inserted 2 in columns 24, 30, or 36.
22. Production workers hired for Area 1 exceed quantity equal to twice plant capacity under construction in Area 1. Number corrected to twice plant capacity under construction or 3 (if no plant is under construction).
23. Production workers hired for Area 2 exceed quantity equal to twice plant capacity under construction in Area 2. Number corrected to twice plant capacity under construction or 3 (if no plant is under construction).
24. Production workers hired for Area 3 exceed quantity equal to twice plant capacity under construction in Area 3. Number corrected to twice plant capacity under construction or 3 (if no plant is under construction).
25. Minimum price of stock for stock issue not specified. Price set at 50 percent of previous quarter's stock price or issuance is denied.
26. Stock retirement price not specified. Price set at 125 percent of previous quarter's stock price.
27. You may have only two bond issues outstanding at any one time. You already have two issues outstanding, and your request is denied.
28. Bond interest not specified. Interest rate set at 2 percent above posted rate for short term interest.
29. Amount of first payment on bond requested not specified. First payment set at 10 percent of amount requested.
30. Quarter for first payment on bond requested not specified. First payment due next quarter.
31. Amount of other payments on bond requested not specified. Amount set at 10 percent of amount requested.
32. Span of payments for bond requested not specified. Payment due quarterly.
33. Quarter in production not specified in sale of plant. Request for sale of plant denied.
34. Area not specified in plant sale. Request for sale of plant denied.
35. Unit capacity in plant sale not specified. Request for sale of plant denied.
36. Area not specified in purchase of plant. Request for purchase of plant denied.
37. Unit capacity not specified in purchase of plant. Request for purchase of plant denied.

Appendix B
Past Operating Statements

GIDGET COMPANY

STATEMENT OF INCOME
JANUARY 1 TO MARCH 31 YEAR 1.

	THIS QUARTER	YEAR TO DATE
1. NET SALES $36. $36. $36.	$ 401040.	$ 401040.
2. MANUFACTURING COST OF GOODS SOLD	255132.	255132.
3. SELLING AND ADMINISTRATIVE EXPENSES	108200.	108200.
4. WAREHOUSE & INVENTORY CARRY. COSTS	25100.	25100.
5. TOTAL OPERATING EXPENSES	$ 388432.	$ 388432.
6. OPERATING INCOME	$ 12608.	$ 12608.
7. NET INTEREST(EXPENSE LESS REVENUE)	6900.	6900.
8. INCOME BEFORE INCOME TAXES	$ 5708.	$ 5708.
9. PROVISION FOR INCOME TAXES (50 PERCENT)	2854.	2854.
10. NET INCOME AFTER TAXES	$ 2854.	$ 2854.
11. DIVIDENDS DECLARED	0.	0.
12. TO RETAINED EARNINGS	$ 2854.	$ 2854.
13. NUMBER OF SHARES OUTSTANDING 100000.		
14. EARNINGS PER SHARE	$ .029	$ .029
15. DIVIDENDS PER SHARE	$ .000	$ .000

PAGE 5
QUARTER 1.

INDUSTRY 22.
TEAM 1

GIDGET COMPANY
STATEMENT OF FINANCIAL POSITION
MARCH 31 YEAR 1.

ASSETS

CURRENT ASSETS
1. CASH $ 33544.
2. ACCOUNTS RECEIVABLE   466257.
3. SHORT TERM INVESTMENTS   0.
   INVENTORIES
4.   RAW MATERIAL $ 14226.
5.   FINISHED GOODS   32292.
6.   TOTAL CURRENT ASSETS $ 46518. $ 546319.

INVESTMENTS
7. PLANTS AND EQUIPMENT AT COST $ 1000000.
8.   LESS ACCUMULATED DEPRECIATION   100000.
9. NET PLANT   900000.

10.   TOTAL ASSETS $ 1446319.

LIABILITIES
CURRENT LIABILITIES
11. NOTES PAYABLE $ 255000.
12. ESTIMATED INCOME TAX PAYABLE   2854.
13. DIVIDENDS PAYABLE   0.
14.   TOTAL CURRENT LIABILITIES $ 257854.

LONG TERM DEBT
15. BONDS PAYABLE   #1   200000.
                          #2   0.   200000.

16.   TOTAL LIABILITIES $ 457854.

STOCKHOLDERS' EQUITY

17. COMMON STOCK (PAR VALUE $10) $ 1000000.
18. ACCUM. RETAINED EARNINGS $ -14390.
19. ADD QUARTER EARNINGS   2854.
20.   TOTAL STOCKHOLDERS' EQUITY   -11536.   988464.

21.   TOTAL LIABILITIES PLUS STOCKHOLDERS' EQUITY $ 1446318.

22. STOCKMARKET PRICE OF STOCK $ 10.14

INDUSTRY 22.
TEAM   1

PAGE 4
QUARTER 2.

GIDGET COMPANY

STATEMENT OF INCOME
APRIL 1 TO JUNE 30 YEAR 1.

		THIS QUARTER	YEAR TO DATE
1.	NET SALES $37. $37. $37.	$ 432012.	$ 833052.
2.	MANUFACTURING COST OF GOODS SOLD	265732.	520864.
3.	SELLING AND ADMINISTRATIVE EXPENSES	87600.	195800.
4.	WAREHOUSE & INVENTORY CARRY. COSTS	23620.	48720.
5.	TOTAL OPERATING EXPENSES	$ 376952.	$ 765384.
6.	OPERATING INCOME	$ 55060.	$ 67668.
7.	NET INTEREST(EXPENSE LESS REVENUE)	11375.	18275.
8.	INCOME BEFORE INCOME TAXES	$ 43685.	$ 49393.
9.	PROVISION FOR INCOME TAXES (50 PERCENT)	21843.	24696.
10.	NET INCOME AFTER TAXES	$ 21843.	$ 24697.
11.	DIVIDENDS DECLARED	0.	0.
12.	TO RETAINED EARNINGS	$ 21843.	$ 24697.
13.	NUMBER OF SHARES OUTSTANDING 100000.		
14.	EARNINGS PER SHARE	$ .218	$ .247
15.	DIVIDENDS PER SHARE	$ .000	$ .000

PAGE 5
QUARTER 2.

INDUSTRY 22.
TEAM 1

GIDGET COMPANY
STATEMENT OF FINANCIAL POSITION
JUNE 30 YEAR 1.

ASSETS

CURRENT ASSETS
1. CASH $ 174487.
2. ACCOUNTS RECEIVABLE   549227.
3. SHORT TERM INVESTMENTS   0.
    INVENTORIES
4. RAW MATERIAL $ 13972.
5. FINISHED GOODS   39464.   53436.
6.   TOTAL CURRENT ASSETS $ 777150.

INVESTMENTS
7. PLANTS AND EQUIPMENT AT COST $ 1300000.
8. LESS ACCUMULATED DEPRECIATION   150000.   1150000.
9. NET PLANT

10.   TOTAL ASSETS $ 1927150.

LIABILITIES
CURRENT LIABILITIES
11. NOTES PAYABLE $ 315000.
12. ESTIMATED INCOME TAX PAYABLE   21843.
13. DIVIDENDS PAYABLE   0.
14.   TOTAL CURRENT LIABILITIES $ 336843.

LONG TERM DEBT
15. BONDS PAYABLE   #1   180000.
                        #2   400000.   580000.

16.   TOTAL LIABILITIES $ 916843.

STOCKHOLDERS' EQUITY

17. COMMON STOCK (PAR VALUE $10) $ 1000000.
18. ACCUM. RETAINED EARNINGS $ -11536.
19. ADD QUARTER EARNINGS   21843.   10307.
20.   TOTAL STOCKHOLDERS' EQUITY $ 1010307.

21.   TOTAL LIABILITIES PLUS STOCKHOLDERS' EQUITY $ 1927149.

22. STOCKMARKET PRICE OF STOCK $ 10.85

PAGE 4
QUARTER 3.

GIDGET COMPANY

STATEMENT OF INCOME
JULY 1 TO SEPTEMBER 30 YEAR 1.

	THIS QUARTER	YEAR TO DATE
1. NET SALES $38. $38. $38.	$ 444638.	$ 1277690.
2. MANUFACTURING COST OF GOODS SOLD	341289.	862153.
3. SELLING AND ADMINISTRATIVE EXPENSES	102400.	298200.
4. WAREHOUSE & INVENTORY CARRY. COSTS	22668.	71388.
5. TOTAL OPERATING EXPENSES	$ 466357.	$ 1231741.
6. OPERATING INCOME	$ -21719.	$ 45949.
7. NET INTEREST(EXPENSE LESS REVENUE)	15469.	33744.
8. INCOME BEFORE INCOME TAXES	$ -37188.	$ 12205.
9. PROVISION FOR INCOME TAXES (50 PERCENT)	0.	24696.
10. NET INCOME AFTER TAXES	$ -37188.	$ -12491.
11. DIVIDENDS DECLARED	0.	0.
12. TO RETAINED EARNINGS	$ -37188.	$ -12491.
13. NUMBER OF SHARES OUTSTANDING 100000.		
14. EARNINGS PER SHARE	$ -.372	$ -.125
15. DIVIDENDS PER SHARE	$ .000	$ .000

INDUSTRY 22.
TEAM   1

PAGE 5
QUARTER 3.

GIDGET COMPANY
STATEMENT OF FINANCIAL POSITION
SEPTEMBER 30 YEAR 1.

ASSETS

CURRENT ASSETS
1. CASH $ 0.
2. ACCOUNTS RECEIVABLE   572979.
3. SHORT TERM INVESTMENTS   0.
   INVENTORIES
4.   RAW MATERIAL $ 0.
5.   FINISHED GOODS   59297.
6.   TOTAL CURRENT ASSETS   59297. $ 632277.

INVESTMENTS
7. PLANTS AND EQUIPMENT AT COST $ 1300000.
8. LESS ACCUMULATED DEPRECIATION   200000.
9. NET PLANT   1100000.

10.   TOTAL ASSETS $ 1732277.

LIABILITIES

CURRENT LIABILITIES
11. NOTES PAYABLE $ 199157.
12. ESTIMATED INCOME TAX PAYABLE   0.
13. DIVIDENDS PAYABLE   0.
14.   TOTAL CURRENT LIABILITIES $ 199157.

LONG TERM DEBT
15. BONDS PAYABLE   #1   160000.
                            #2   400000.   560000.

16.   TOTAL LIABILITIES $ 759157.

STOCKHOLDERS' EQUITY

17. COMMON STOCK (PAR VALUE $10) $ 1000000.
18. ACCUM. RETAINED EARNINGS $ 10307.
19. ADD QUARTER EARNINGS   -37188.   -26881.
20.   TOTAL STOCKHOLDERS' EQUITY   973119.

21.   TOTAL LIABILITIES PLUS STOCKHOLDERS'EQUITY $ 1732277.

22. STOCKMARKET PRICE OF STOCK $ 9.78

GIDGET COMPANY

STATEMENT OF INCOME
OCTOBER 1 TO DECEMBER 31 YEAR 1.

		THIS QUARTER	YEAR TO DATE
1.	NET SALES $37. $37. $37.	$ 525585.	$ 1803275.
2.	MANUFACTURING COST OF GOODS SOLD	316312.	1178465.
3.	SELLING AND ADMINISTRATIVE EXPENSES	111000.	409200.
4.	WAREHOUSE & INVENTORY CARRY. COSTS	30466.	101854.
5.	TOTAL OPERATING EXPENSES	$ 457778.	$ 1689519.
6.	OPERATING INCOME	$ 67807.	$ 113756.
7.	NET INTEREST(EXPENSE LESS REVENUE)	25779.	59523.
8.	INCOME BEFORE INCOME TAXES	$ 42028.	$ 54233.
9.	PROVISION FOR INCOME TAXES (50 PERCENT)	2421.A	27116.
10.	NET INCOME AFTER TAXES	$ 39608.	$ 27117.
11.	DIVIDENDS DECLARED	0.	0.
12.	TO RETAINED EARNINGS	$ 39608.	$ 27117.
13.	NUMBER OF SHARES OUTSTANDING 100000.		
14.	EARNINGS PER SHARE	$ .396	$ .271
15.	DIVIDENDS PER SHARE	$ .000	$ .000

A - TAX BASED ON INCOME AFTER LOSS CARRY FORWARD

GIDGET COMPANY
STATEMENT OF FINANCIAL POSITION
DECEMBER 31 YEAR 1.

ASSETS

CURRENT ASSETS
1. CASH $ 102208.
2. ACCOUNTS RECEIVABLE   650882.
3. SHORT TERM INVESTMENTS   0.
   INVENTORIES
4.   RAW MATERIAL $ 35930.
5.   FINISHED GOODS   40705.   76635.
6.   TOTAL CURRENT ASSETS $ 829725.

INVESTMENTS
7. PLANTS AND EQUIPMENT AT COST $ 1300000.
8. LESS ACCUMULATED DEPRECIATION   265000.
9. NET PLANT   1035000.

10.   TOTAL ASSETS $ 1864725.

          LIABILITIES

CURRENT LIABILITIES
11. NOTES PAYABLE $ 349578.
12. ESTIMATED INCOME TAX PAYABLE   2421.
13. DIVIDENDS PAYABLE   0.
14.   TOTAL CURRENT LIABILITIES $ 351999.

LONG TERM DEBT
15. BONDS PAYABLE   #1   140000.
                        #2   360000.   500000.

16.   TOTAL LIABILITIES $ 851999.

    STOCKHOLDERS' EQUITY

17. COMMON STOCK (PAR VALUE $10) $ 1000000.
18. ACCUM. RETAINED EARNINGS $ -26881.
19. ADD QUARTER EARNINGS   39608.   12727.
20.   TOTAL STOCKHOLDERS' EQUITY   1012727.

21.   TOTAL LIABILITIES PLUS STOCKHOLDERS'EQUITY $ 1864725.

22. STOCKMARKET PRICE OF STOCK $ 11.02

DECISION SHEET for TEMPOMATIC IV (DO NOT PUNCH DECIMAL POINTS; PLACE LAST DIGIT OF EACH DECISION IN RIGHT COLUMN OF BOX)

CARD 1

Natl. Adv. No. Pgs.	8
Local Advertising-Number Pgs. — Area 1	8
Local Advertising-Number Pgs. — Area 2	3
Local Advertising-Number Pgs. — Area 3	2
No. of Prod. Improvement	7 2 0
Sales Price Per Unit — Area 1	2
Sales Price Per Unit — Area 2	
Sales Price Per Unit — Area 3	
Company Name	GIDGET
Ind'v Number	2 2
Company Number + 50	5 1

CARD 2

Quarter	5
Number of Salespersons Hired — Area 1	4 5 0 0
Number of Salespersons Hired — Area 2	3 5 0 0
Number of Salespersons Hired — Area 3	8 0 0 0
Number of Salespersons Discharged	8 0 0 0
Units Transferred From — Total Trfd. / Area 1	
Units Transferred To — Area 2	
Units Transferred To — Area 3	
Company Name	GIDGET
Co. No.	1 0 2

CARD 3

Material Ordered-Units — Area 1	1 0 0 0 0
Material Ordered-Units — Area 2	
Material Ordered-Units — Area 3	
Total S-T Loan Repayment-$	5 0 0 0 0
Short-Term Loan Requested-$	
Plant Ordered Constructed-Units — Area 1, 2, 3	
% of Profit to Dividend	
Dividend Per Share-¢	
Cost of Environment Information (A B C D E F G H I)	1 1 1 1 1
Co. No.	1 0 3

CARD 4

Total Actual Production-Units — Area 1	1 5 6 0 0
Total Actual Production-Units — Area 2	
Total Actual Production-Units — Area 3	
Production Workers Hired-Number — Area 1	1
Production Workers Hired-Number — Area 2, 3	
Production Workers Discharged-Number — Area 1, 2, 3	
Short-Term Investment — Number	
Deposit-$	
Withdraw-$	
Worker Layoffs (A1 A2 A3)	
Cost	
Co. No.	1 0 4

CARD 5

Stock Retired-Share-¢ — Number	
Stock Retired-Share-¢ — Price	
Stock Issue-Share-¢ — Number	
Stock Issue-Share-¢ — Price	
Amount $	4 0 0 0 0 0
Interest-% per yr. × 100	9 0 0
Amount of 1st Payment	4 0 0 0 0
Qtr. of 1st Pay.	6
Freq. of Pay.	4 0 0 0 0
Amount of Other Payment	
Extra Payment 1st Bond	1 1 2 0 0 0 0
Co. No.	1 0 5

Bonds: Issuance and Payment

CARD 6

Reg. Pay $/Qtr.	2 4 0 0
Overtime ¢/Unit	1 5 0 0
Hiring Cost $/Person	3 0 0 0
Material Cost: Change to ($)	1 4 0 0 0 0
Sale Price $	5 0 0 0 0
Med. Price	
Low Price	
High Price — Sale of Plant — Area	1
Accumulated Depreciation / Capacity-Units	2 0 0 0
Purchase Price $	2 2 0 0 0 0
Purchase of Plant — Area	1
Capacity-Units	2 0 0 0
Co. No.	1 0 6
Option	

Prod. Worker Pay: Change to ($)

© 1984 by Houghton Mifflin Company

TEMPOMATIC IV: A MANAGEMENT SIMULATION BY CHARLES R. SCOTT JR. AND ALONZO J. STRICKLAND III
COPYRIGHT HOUGHTON MIFFLIN, 1984 (RELEASE C1)

GIDGET COMPANY

PAGE 1   INDUSTRY 22.
QUARTER 5.   TEAM 1

PRODUCTION ANALYSIS
JANUARY 1 TO MARCH 31 YEAR 2.

MATERIAL	AREA 1 UNITS	$/UNIT	COST	AREA 2 UNITS	$/UNIT	COST	AREA 3 UNITS	$/UNIT	COST	TOTAL UNITS	TOTAL COST
1. BEG. INV.	6000.	$ 5.99	$ 35930.	0.	$ .00	$ 0.	0.	$ .00	$ 0.	6000.	$ 35930.
2. RECEIPTS	20000.	$ 6.00	$ 120000.	0.	$ .00	$ 0.	0.	$ .00	$ 0.	20000.	$ 120000.
3. AVAILABLE	26000.	$ 6.00	$ 155930.	0.	$ .00	$ 0.	0.	$ .00	$ 0.	26000.	$ 155930.
4. USAGE	15600.	$ 6.00	$ 93636.	0.	$ .00	$ 0.	0.	$ .00	$ 0.	15600.	$ 93636.
5. FINAL INV.	10400.	$ 5.99	$ 62294.	0.	$ .00	$ 0.	0.	$ .00	$ 0.	10400.	$ 62294.
6. REC.-NEXT QTR	10000.	$ 7.00	$ 70000.	0.	$ .00	$ 0.	0.	$ .00	$ 0.	10000.	$ 70000.
7. AVAIL.-NEXT QT	20400.	$ 6.49	$ 132294.	0.	$ .00	$ 0.	0.	$ .00	$ 0.	20400.	$ 132294.

8. CARRY. COST ($ 1.00 X (1)) $ 6000.
9. TOT. MAT. COST (4) + (8) $ 99636.

WORK FORCE — THIS QUARTER

WORK FORCE	AREA 1	AREA 2	AREA 3	TOTAL
10. NO. WORKERS BEG. QTR.	41.	0.	0.	41.
11. WORKERS DISCHARGED	0.	0.	0.	
12. WORKERS LOST TO T'OVER	2.	0.	0.	2.
13. WORKERS LAID OFF	0.	0.	0.	0.
14. WORKERS AVAILABLE	39.	0.	0.	39.
15. CREWS AVAILABLE(CREW = 3)	13.	0.	0.	13.
16. WORKERS HIRED	1.	0.	0.	1.
17. CREW PRODUCTIVITY	1000.	1000.	1000.	1000.
18. MAX. PROD. W/O O'TIME	13000.	0.	0.	13000.
19. PLANT CAP. AVAIL.,UN.	13000.	0.	0.	13000.
20. PLANT UNDER CON.,UN.	0.	0.	0.	
21. PLANT ORDERED,UNITS	0.	0.	0.	

WORK FORCE — NEXT QUARTER

WORK FORCE	AREA 1	AREA 2	AREA 3	TOTAL
10. NO. WORKERS BEG. QTR.	40.	0.	0.	40.
12. WORKERS LOST TO T'OVER	2.	0.	0.	2.
14. WORKERS AVAILABLE	38.	0.	0.	38.
15. CREWS AVAILABLE(CREW = 3)	12.	0.	0.	12.
17. CREW PRODUCTIVITY	1000.	1000.	1000.	1000.
18. MAX. PROD. W/O O'TIME	12000.	0.	0.	12000.
19. PLANT CAP. AVAIL.,UN.	13000.	0.	0.	13000.
21. PLANT ORDERED,UNITS	0.			

MFG. COST OF GOODS SOLD — THIS QUARTER

		COST	TOTAL COST
1. MATERIAL			$ 99636.
2. LABOR-REG. PAY	($ 2400. X 40.)	$ 96000.	
3. LAYOFF COST	($ 0. X 0.)	0.	
4. OVER TIME PAY	($ 15.00 X 2600.)	39000.	
5. HIRING COST	($ 3000. X 1.)	3000.	
6. OVERHEAD	($138000.X 50$)		69000.
7. DEPRECIATION			65000.

	UNITS	$/UNIT	TOTAL COST
8. TOTAL MFG. COST	15600.	$ 23.82	$ 371636.
9. BEG. FIN. GOODS INV.	1828.	22.27	40705.
10. TOTAL COST OF GOODS	17428.	23.66	412341.
11. END FIN. GOODS INV.	2688.	23.66	63597.
12. MFG. COST OF GOODS SOLD	14740.	$ 23.66	$ 348744.

MFG. COST OF GOODS SOLD — NEXT QUARTER

	UNITS	$/UNITS	TOTAL COST
	2688.	$ 23.66	$ 63597.

GIDGET COMPANY

WAREHOUSE OPERATIONS
JANUARY 1 TO MARCH 31 YEAR 2.

PAGE 2
QUARTER 5.

INDUSTRY 22.
TEAM 1

| | THIS QUARTER | | | | NEXT QUARTER | | | |
	AREA 1	AREA 2	AREA 3	TOTAL	AREA 1	AREA 2	AREA 3	TOTAL
1. BEGINNING INVENTORY	282.	1101.	445.	1828.	0.	1502.	1186.	2688.
2. UNITS ASSEMBLED	15600.	0.	0.	15600.				
3. UNITS AVAILABLE	15882.	1101.	445.	17428.				
4. TRANSFER OF UNITS TO	0.	4500.	3500.	8000.				
5. TRANSFER OF UNITS FROM	8000.	0.	0.	8000.				
6. UNITS AVAILABLE FOR SALE	7882.	5601.	3945.	17428.				
7. UNITS SOLD	7882.	4099.	2759.	14740.				
8. ENDING INVENTORY	0.	1502.	1186.	2688.				
9. UNITS OF SALES LOST	754.	0.	0.	0.				

WAREHOUSE AND FINISHED GOODS EXPENSE

10. COST OF UNITS TRANSFERRED		$ 32000.
11. COST OF CARRYING INVENTORY ($2.00 PER UNIT X 1828.) $ 3656. ($2.00 PER UNIT X 2688.)$ 5376.		
12. TOTAL COST OF WAREHOUSE OPERATIONS		35656.

SELLING AND ADMINISTRATIVE EXPENSE ANALYSIS

DESCRIPTION	AREA 1	2	3	TOTAL	RATE	EXPENSES	NEXT QTR. EXP.
1. SALES PERSONS HIRED (HIRING COST= $ 1100.)				0.	$ 4500.	$ 0.	0.
2. SALES PERSONS IN TRAINING	7.	2.	2.	3.	3400.	10200.	13.
3. REGULAR SALES PERSONS				11.	3400.	37400.	
4. TOTAL PERSONS IN SALES				14.	3400.	$ 47600.	
5. NATIONAL ADVERTISING (PAGES)	8.	3.	2.	8.	2800.	22400.	
6. LOCAL ADVERTISING (PAGES)				13.	900.	11700.	
7. PRODUCT IMPROVEMENTS				0.	10000.	0.	
8. MARKET INFORMATION						10000.	
9. ADMINISTRATIVE EXPENSES						25000.	
10. TOTAL SELLING AND ADMINISTRATIVE EXPENSE						$ 116700.	$ 44200.

11. LOST SALES PERSONS (FOR NEXT QTR.)   1.

GIDGET COMPANY

CASH FLOW STATEMENT
JANUARY 1 TO MARCH 31 YEAR 2.

PAGE 3   INDUSTRY 22.
QUARTER 5.   TEAM 1

	THIS QTR.	NEXT QTR.(ESTIMATED)
CASH RECEIPTS		
1. CASH ON HAND BEGIN QTR.	$ 102208.	$ 131699.
2. COLLECTION OF ACCOUNTS RECEIVABLE	496659.	490294.
3. STOCK, BOND, PLANT SALES INCOME	400000.	140000.
4. TOTAL CASH AVAILABLE	$ 998867.	$ 761993. (PLUS 10 PERCENT OF NEXT QUARTER'S SALES)
CASH PAYMENTS		
5. MATERIAL PURCHASES	$ 126000.	$ 80400.
6. NET SHORT TERM INTEREST	9613.	4812.
7. INTEREST ON BONDS PAYABLE	15200.	16200. (INTEREST RATE = 11.00 %)
8. DECLARED DIVIDENDS PAID	0.	0.
9. INCOME TAX PAID	2421.	17104.
10. BOND AND STOCK RETIREMENT	180000.	80000.
11. PAYMENTS ON PLANT	0.	220000.
12. SHORT TERM LOAN + INVEST. PAYMENTS	224578.	150000.
13. LABOR + VARIABLE OVERHEAD	207000.	?
14. WAREHOUSE AND INVENTORY CARRY. COST	35656.	?
15. SELLING AND ADMINISTRATIVE EXPENSE	116700.	?
16. TOTAL CASH PAYMENTS	917168.	568516. (PLUS DISCRETIONARY CASH PAYMENTS)
17. NET CASH BALANCE	$ 81699.	$ 193477.
18. SHORT TERM LOAN	50000.	
19. CASH BALANCE AT END OF QTR.	$ 131699.	$ 193477. (BEFORE DISCRETIONARY CASH PAYMENTS)
20. ADDED INTEREST (INCLUDED IN LINE 6)	0.	

NOTE: THE 2000. UNIT PLANT SOLD IN AREA 1. FOR $ 140000.
ORIGINALY COST $ 200000. , BUT HAD ACCUMULATED DEPRECIATION
OF $ 50000. THUS, THERE WAS A GAIN (OR LOSS) OF $ -10000.
($ 140000. + $ 50000. - $ 200000.) THE GAIN (OR LOSS) WILL
BE CHARGED TO YOUR QUARTER 6. RETAINED EARNINGS

GIDGET COMPANY

STATEMENT OF INCOME
JANUARY 1 TO MARCH 31 YEAR 2.

		THIS QUARTER	YEAR TO DATE
1.	NET SALES $38. $38. $38.	$ 560120.	$ 560120.
2.	MANUFACTURING COST OF GOODS SOLD	348744.	348744.
3.	SELLING AND ADMINISTRATIVE EXPENSES	116700.	116700.
4.	WAREHOUSE & INVENTORY CARRY. COSTS	35656.	35656.
5.	TOTAL OPERATING EXPENSES	$ 501100.	$ 501100.
6.	OPERATING INCOME	$ 59020.	$ 59020.
7.	NET INTEREST(EXPENSE LESS REVENUE)	24813.	24813.
8.	INCOME BEFORE INCOME TAXES	$ 34207.	$ 34207.
9.	PROVISION FOR INCOME TAXES (50 PERCENT)	17103.	17103.
10.	NET INCOME AFTER TAXES	$ 17104.	$ 17104.
11.	DIVIDENDS DECLARED	0.	0.
12.	TO RETAINED EARNINGS	$ 17104.	$ 17104.
13.	NUMBER OF SHARES OUTSTANDING 100000.		
14.	EARNINGS PER SHARE	$ .171	$ .171
15.	DIVIDENDS PER SHARE	$ .000	$ .000

PAGE 5
QUARTER 5.

INDUSTRY 22.
TEAM 1

GIDGET COMPANY
STATEMENT OF FINANCIAL POSITION
MARCH 31 YEAR 2.

ASSETS

CURRENT ASSETS
1. CASH $ 131699.
2. ACCOUNTS RECEIVABLE   714342.
3. SHORT TERM INVESTMENTS   0.
INVENTORIES
4.   RAW MATERIAL $ 62294.
5.   FINISHED GOODS   63597.   125891.
6.   TOTAL CURRENT ASSETS $ 971932.

INVESTMENTS
7. PLANTS AND EQUIPMENT AT COST $ 1520000.
8. LESS ACCUMULATED DEPRECIATION   330000.
9. NET PLANT   1190000.

10.   TOTAL ASSETS $ 2161932.

            LIABILITIES
CURRENT LIABILITIES
11. NOTES PAYABLE $ 395000.
12. ESTIMATED INCOME TAX PAYABLE   17104.
13. DIVIDENDS PAYABLE   0.
14.   TOTAL CURRENT LIABILITIES $ 412104.

LONG TERM DEBT
15. BONDS PAYABLE   #1   320000.
                        #2   400000.   720000.

16.   TOTAL LIABILITIES $ 1132104.

            STOCKHOLDERS' EQUITY
17. COMMON STOCK (PAR VALUE $10) $ 1000000.
18. ACCUM. RETAINED EARNINGS $ 12727.
19. ADD QUARTER EARNINGS   17104.
20.   TOTAL STOCKHOLDERS' EQUITY   1029831.

21.   TOTAL LIABILITIES PLUS STOCKHOLDERS'EQUITY $ 2161934.

22. STOCKMARKET PRICE OF STOCK $ 11.58

DECISION SHEET for TEMPOMATIC IV (DO NOT PUNCH DECIMAL POINTS; PLACE LAST DIGIT OF EACH DECISION IN RIGHT COLUMN OF BOX)

CARD 1

Natl. Adv. No. Pgs.	Local Advertising–Number Pgs.			No. of Prod. Improvement	Sales Price Per Unit			Company Name	Ind'y Number	Company Number + 50
	Area 1	Area 2	Area 3		Area 1	Area 2	Area 3			
8	8	3	2	7	3			GIDGET	22	51
					0	39	3			

CARD 2

Number of Salespersons Hired	Number of Salespersons Discharged	Number of Salespersons			Units Transferred To		Total Trfd.	Units Transferred From	Company Name	Co. No.
		Area 1	Area 2	Area 3	Area 1	Area 2	Area 3	Area 1	Area 2	Area 3
6					4000	2500	6800	6800	GIDGET	102

CARD 3

Material Ordered—Units			Plant Ordered Constructed—Units			Short-Term Loan Requested–$	Total S-T Loan Repayment–$	% of Profit to Dividend	Dividend Per Share–¢	Cost of Environment Information	A B C D E F G H I Environment Information	Co. No.
Area 1	Area 2	Area 3	Area 1	Area 2	Area 3							
100000			5000			150000				100000	111111	103

CARD 4

Total Actual Production—Units			Production Workers Hired—Number			Production Workers Discharged—Number		Short-Term Investment	Deposit–$	Withdraw–$	Worker Layoffs	Co. No.
Area 1	Area 2	Area 3	Area 1	Area 2	Area 3						A1 A2 A3 Cost	
114500	4											104

CARD 5

Stock Issue–Share/¢	Number	Stock Retired–Share/¢	Price	Amount $	Interest% per yr. × 100	Amount of 1st Payment	Qtr. of 1st Pay.	Amount of Other Payment	Freq. of Pay.	Extra Pay-ment 1st Bond	Per Crew	Crew Size	Salary $/per.	Hiring $/per.	Co. No.
Number											Productivity		Salespersons		
															105

Bonds: Issuance and Payment

CARD 6

Reg. Pay $/Qtr.	Overtime ¢/Unit	Hiring Cost $/Person	Min. Price	Number	High Price	Med. Price	Low Price	Sale Price $	Accumulated Depreciation	Area	Purchase Price $	Area	Capacity-Units	Option	Co. No.
			Stock Retired–Share/¢					Sale of Plant			Purchase of Plant				106

Material Cost: Change to ($)

Prod. Worker Pay: Change to ($)

TEMPOMATIC IV: A MANAGEMENT SIMULATION BY CHARLES R. SCOTT JR. AND ALONZO J. STRICKLAND III
COPYRIGHT HOUGHTON MIFFLIN, 1984 (RELEASE C1)

GIDGET COMPANY

PAGE 1   INDUSTRY 22.
QUARTER 6.   TEAM 1

PRODUCTION ANALYSIS
APRIL 1 TO JUNE 30 YEAR 2.

MATERIAL	AREA 1 UNITS	$/UNIT	COST	AREA 2 UNITS	$/UNIT	COST	AREA 3 UNITS	$/UNIT	COST	TOTAL UNITS	COST
1. BEG. INV.	10400.	$ 5.99	$ 62294.	0.	$ .00	$ 0.	0.	$ .00	$ 0.	10400.	$ 62294.
2. RECEIPTS	10000.	$ 7.00	$ 70000.	0.	$ .00	$ 0.	0.	$ .00	$ 0.	10000.	$ 70000.
3. AVAILABLE	20400.	$ 6.49	$ 132294.	0.	$ .00	$ 0.	0.	$ .00	$ 0.	20400.	$ 132294.
4. USAGE	14400.	$ 6.49	$ 93456.	0.	$ .00	$ 0.	0.	$ .00	$ 0.	14400.	$ 93456.
5. FINAL INV.	6000.	$ 6.47	$ 38838.	0.	$ .00	$ 0.	0.	$ .00	$ 0.	6000.	$ 38838.
6. REC.-NEXT QTR	10000.	$ 7.00	$ 70000.	0.	$ .00	$ 0.	0.	$ .00	$ 0.	10000.	$ 70000.
7. AVAIL.-NEXT QT	16000.	$ 6.80	$ 108838.	0.	$ .00	$ 0.	0.	$ .00	$ 0.	16000.	$ 108838.

8. CARRY. COST ($ 1.00 X (1)) $ 10400.
9. TOT. MAT. COST (4) + (8) $ 103856.

WORK FORCE	THIS QUARTER AREA 1	AREA 2	AREA 3	TOTAL	NEXT QUARTER AREA 1	AREA 2	AREA 3	TOTAL
10. NO. WORKERS BEG. QTR.	40.	0.	0.	40.	41.	0.	0.	41.
11. WORKERS DISCHARGED	0.	0.	0.	0.				
12. WORKERS LOST TO T'OVER	3.	0.	0.	3.	2.	0.	0.	2.
13. WORKERS LAID OFF	0.	0.	0.	0.				
14. WORKERS AVAILABLE	37.	0.	0.	37.	39.	0.	0.	39.
15. CREWS AVAILABLE (CREW = 3)	12.	0.	0.	12.	13.	0.	0.	13.
16. WORKERS HIRED	4.	0.	0.	4.				
17. CREW PRODUCTIVITY	1000.	1000.	1000.	1000.	1000.	1000.	1000.	1000.
18. MAX. PROD. W/O O'TIME	12000.	0.	0.	12000.	13000.	0.	0.	13000.
19. PLANT CAP. AVAIL.,UN.	13000.	0.	0.	13000.	13000.	0.	0.	13000.
20. PLANT UNDER CON.,UN.	0.	0.	0.	0.				
21. PLANT ORDERED, UNITS	5000.	0.	0.	5000.				

MFG. COST OF GOODS SOLD

	THIS QUARTER		NEXT QUARTER	
1. MATERIAL		$ 103856.		
2. LABOR-REG. PAY	($ 2400. X 41.)	$ 98400.		
3. LAYOFF COST	($ 0. X 0.)	0.		
4. OVER TIME PAY	($ 15.00 X 2400.)	36000.		
5. HIRING COST	($ 3000. X 4.)	12000.		
6. OVERHEAD	($146400. X 50%)	146400.		
7. DEPRECIATION		73200.		
		66000.		

	UNITS	$/UNIT	TOTAL COST	UNITS	$/UNITS	TOTAL COST
8. TOTAL MFG. COST	14400.	$ 27.05	$ 389456.			
9. BEG. FIN. GOODS INV.	2688.	23.66	63597.	721.	$ 26.51	$ 19116.
10. TOTAL COST OF GOODS	17088.	26.51	453053.			
11. END FIN. GOODS INV.	721.	26.51	19116.			
12. MFG. COST OF GOODS SOLD	16367.	$ 26.51	$ 433937.			

GIDGET COMPANY

PAGE 2
QUARTER 6.

INDUSTRY 22.
TEAM 1

WAREHOUSE OPERATIONS
APRIL 1 TO JUNE 30 YEAR 2.

	THIS QUARTER AREA 1	AREA 2	AREA 3	TOTAL	NEXT QUARTER AREA 1	AREA 2	AREA 3	TOTAL
1. BEGINNING INVENTORY	0.	1502.	1186.	2688.	719.	2.	0.	721.
2. UNITS ASSEMBLED	14400.	0.	0.	14400.				
3. UNITS AVAILABLE	14400.	1502.	1186.	17088.				
4. TRANSFER OF UNITS TO	0.	4000.	2500.	6500.				
5. TRANSFER OF UNITS FROM	6500.	0.	0.	6500.				
6. UNITS AVAILABLE FOR SALE	7900.	5502.	3686.	17088.				
7. UNITS SOLD	7181.	5500.	3686.	16367.				
8. ENDING INVENTORY	719.	2.	0.	721.				
9. UNITS OF SALES LOST	0.	0.	452.					

WAREHOUSE AND FINISHED GOODS EXPENSE

10. COST OF UNITS TRANSFERRED		$ 26000.
11. COST OF CARRYING INVENTORY ($4.00 PER UNIT X 2688.)	($4.00 PER UNIT X 721.)$ 2884.	$ 10752.
12. TOTAL COST OF WAREHOUSE OPERATIONS		36752.

SELLING AND ADMINISTRATIVE EXPENSE ANALYSIS

DESCRIPTION	AREA 1	2	3	TOTAL	RATE	EXPENSES	NEXT QTR. EXP.
1. SALES PERSONS HIRED (HIRING COST= $ 1100.)				0.	$ 4500.	$ 0.	0.
2. SALES PERSONS IN TRAINING				0.	3400.	0.	12.
3. REGULAR SALES PERSONS	7.	3.	3.	13.	3400.	44200.	
4. TOTAL PERSONS IN SALES				13.	3400.	$ 44200.	$ 40800.
5. NATIONAL ADVERTISING (PAGES)				8.	2800.	22400.	
6. LOCAL ADVERTISING (PAGES)	8.	3.	2.	13.	900.	11700.	
7. PRODUCT IMPROVEMENTS				0.	10000.	0.	
8. MARKET INFORMATION						12000.	
9. ADMINISTRATIVE EXPENSES						25000.	
10. TOTAL SELLING AND ADMINISTRATIVE EXPENSE						$ 115300.	

11. LOST SALES PERSONS (FOR NEXT QTR.)   1.

GIDGET COMPANY

PAGE 3
QUARTER 6.

INDUSTRY 22.
TEAM 1

CASH FLOW STATEMENT
APRIL 1 TO JUNE 30 YEAR 2.

CASH RECEIPTS

		THIS QTR.	NEXT QTR. (ESTIMATED)
1.	CASH ON HAND BEGIN QTR.	$ 131699.	$ 0.
2.	COLLECTION OF ACCOUNTS RECEIVABLE	554125.	543204.
3.	STOCK, BOND, PLANT SALES INCOME	140000.	0.
4.	TOTAL CASH AVAILABLE	$ 825824.	$ 543204. (PLUS 10 PERCENT OF NEXT QUARTER'S SALES)

CASH PAYMENTS

5.	MATERIAL PURCHASES	$ 80400.	$ 76000.
6.	NET SHORT TERM INTEREST	4812.	15098. (INTEREST RATE = 11.50 %)
7.	INTEREST ON BONDS PAYABLE	16200.	14400.
8.	DECLARED DIVIDENDS PAID	0.	0.
9.	INCOME TAX PAID	17104.	15656.
10.	BOND AND STOCK RETIREMENT	80000.	80000.
11.	PAYMENTS ON PLANT	320000.	400000.
12.	SHORT TERM LOAN + INVEST. PAYMENTS	150000.	132172.
13.	LABOR + VARIABLE OVERHEAD	219600.	?
14.	WAREHOUSE AND INVENTORY CARRY. COST	36752.	?
15.	SELLING AND ADMINISTRATIVE EXPENSE	115300.	?
16.	TOTAL CASH PAYMENTS	1040168.	733325. (PLUS DISCRETIONARY CASH PAYMENTS)

17.	NET CASH BALANCE	$ -214344.	$ -190121.
18.	SHORT TERM LOAN	214344.	
19.	CASH BALANCE AT END OF QTR.	$ 0.	$ -190121. (BEFORE DISCRETIONARY CASH PAYMENTS)
20.	ADDED INTEREST (INCLUDED IN LINE 6)		8217.

GIDGET COMPANY

STATEMENT OF INCOME
APRIL 1 TO JUNE 30 YEAR 2.

		THIS QUARTER	YEAR TO DATE
1.	NET SALES $39. $39. $39.	$ 638313.	$ 1198433.
2.	MANUFACTURING COST OF GOODS SOLD	433937.	782681.
3.	SELLING AND ADMINISTRATIVE EXPENSES	115300.	232000.
4.	WAREHOUSE & INVENTORY CARRY. COSTS	36752.	72408.
5.	TOTAL OPERATING EXPENSES	$ 585989.	$ 1087089.
6.	OPERATING INCOME	$ 52324.	$ 111344.
7.	NET INTEREST(EXPENSE LESS REVENUE)	21012.	45825.
8.	INCOME BEFORE INCOME TAXES	$ 31312.	$ 65519.
9.	PROVISION FOR INCOME TAXES (50 PERCENT)	15656.	32758.
10.	NET INCOME AFTER TAXES	$ 15656.	$ 32761.
11.	DIVIDENDS DECLARED	0.	0.
12.	TO RETAINED EARNINGS	$ 15656.	$ 32761.
13.	NUMBER OF SHARES OUTSTANDING 100000.		
14.	EARNINGS PER SHARE	$ .157	$ .328
15.	DIVIDENDS PER SHARE	$ .000	$ .000

GIDGET COMPANY
STATEMENT OF FINANCIAL POSITION
JUNE 30 YEAR 2.

ASSETS

CURRENT ASSETS
1. CASH .... $ 0.
2. ACCOUNTS RECEIVABLE .... 798530.
3. SHORT TERM INVESTMENTS .... 0.
   INVENTORIES
4.   RAW MATERIAL .... $ 38838.
5.   FINISHED GOODS .... 19116. $ 57954.
6.   TOTAL CURRENT ASSETS .... $ 856484.

INVESTMENTS
7. PLANTS AND EQUIPMENT AT COST .... $ 1820000.
8.   LESS ACCUMULATED DEPRECIATION .... 346000.
9. NET PLANT .... 1474000.

10.   TOTAL ASSETS .... $ 2330483.

LIABILITIES
CURRENT LIABILITIES
11. NOTES PAYABLE .... $ 639344.
12. ESTIMATED INCOME TAX PAYABLE .... 15656.
13. DIVIDENDS PAYABLE .... 0. $ 655000.
14.   TOTAL CURRENT LIABILITIES

LONG TERM DEBT
15. BONDS PAYABLE   #1   280000.
                           #2   360000.   640000.

16.   TOTAL LIABILITIES .... $ 1295000.

STOCKHOLDERS' EQUITY

17. COMMON STOCK (PAR VALUE $10) .... $ 1000000.
18. ACCUM. RETAINED EARNINGS .... $ 19831.
19. ADD QUARTER EARNINGS .... 15656.   35487.
20.   TOTAL STOCKHOLDERS' EQUITY   1035487.

21.   TOTAL LIABILITIES PLUS STOCKHOLDERS'EQUITY $ 2330486.

22. STOCKMARKET PRICE OF STOCK .... $ 12.10

DECISION SHEET for TEMPOMATIC IV (DO NOT PUNCH DECIMAL POINTS; PLACE LAST DIGIT OF EACH DECISION IN RIGHT COLUMN OF BOX)

CARD 1

1 2 3 4	5 6 7 8	9 10 11 12 13 14 15 16 17 18 19 20 21 22 23 24 25 26	27 28 29 30 31 32 33 34 35	36 37 38 39 40 41 42 43 44	45 46 47 48 49 50 51 52 53 54	55 56 57 58 59 60 61 62 63 64 65 66	67 68 69 70 71 72 73 74 75 76	77 78	79 80
8	8	4 3	7	2	0	4 0	G I D G E T	2 2	5 1
Natl. Adv. No. Pgs.	Area 1	Area 2	Area 3	No. of Prod. Improvement	Area 1	Area 2	Area 3	Ind'y Number	Company Number + 50
		Local Advertising–Number Pgs.				Sales Price Per Unit	Company Name		
			Number of Salespersons						

CARD 2

1 2 3 4 5 6 7 8	9 10 11 12 13 14 15 16 17 18 19 20 21 22 23 24 25 26	27 28 29 30 31 32 33 34 35 36 37 38 39 40 41 42 43 44	45 46 47 48 49 50 51 52 53 54 55 56 57 58 59 60 61 62	63 64 65 66 67 68 69 70 71 72 73 74 75 76	77 78	79 80
7 2	4 5 0 0	3 0 0 0	7 5 0 0	7 5 0 0	1 0	2
Quarter	Area 1	Area 2	Area 3	Total Trfd.	Co. No.	
Number of Salespersons Hired		Units Transferred To		Units Transferred From	Company Name	G I D G E T
Number of Salespersons Discharged						

CARD 3

1 2 3 4 5 6	7 8 9 10 11 12 13 14 15 16 17 18 19 20 21 22 23 24	25 26 27 28 29 30 31 32 33 34 35 36 37 38 39 40 41 42 43 44	45 46 47 48 49 50 51 52 53 54	55 56 57 58 59 60 61 62 63 64 65 66	67 68 69 70 71 72 73 74 75 76	77 78	79 80
2 0 0 0 0	1 7				8 5 0 0	4 1	1 0 3
Area 1	Area 2	Area 3	Short-Term Loan Requested–$	Total S-T Loan Repayment–$	% of Profit to Dividend	Dividend Per Share–¢	Cost of Environment Information	A B C D E F G H I Environment Information	Co. No.
	Material Ordered–Units		Plant Ordered Constructed–Units						

CARD 4

1 2 3 4 5 6	7 8 9 10 11 12 13 14 15 16 17 18 19 20	21 22 23 24 25 26 27 28 29 30 31 32 33 34 35 36 37 38 39 40	41 42 43 44 45 46 47 48 49 50 51 52	53 54 55 56 57 58 59 60 61 62 63 64	65 66 67 68 69 70 71 72 73 74 75 76	77 78	79 80
1 5 6 0 0						A1 A2 A3	1 0 4
Area 1	Area 2	Area 3	Area 1	Area 2	Area 3	Withdraw–$	Deposit–$	Worker Layoffs	Cost	Co. No.
Total Actual Production–Units			Production Workers Hired–Number		Production Workers Discharged–Number	Short-Term Investment				

CARD 5

1 2 3 4 5 6	7 8 9 10 11 12 13 14 15 16 17 18 19 20 21 22 23	24 25 26 27 28 29 30 31 32 33 34 35 36	37 38 39 40 41 42 43 44 45 46 47 48 49	50 51 52 53 54	55 56 57 58 59 60 61 62 63 64 65 66	67 68 69 70 71 72 73 74 75 76	77 78	79 80
4 0 0 0 0	1 2 0 0							1 0 5
Number	Min. Price	Number	Price	Amount $	Interest % per yr. × 100	Amount of 1st Payment	Qtr. of 1st Pay.	Freq. of Pay.	Amount of Other Payment	Extra Pay-ment 1st Bond	Per Crew	Crew Size	Salary $/per.	Hiring $/per.	Co. No.
Stock Issue–Share/¢		Stock Retired–Share/¢			Bonds: Issuance and Payment						Productivity		Salespersons		

CARD 6

1 2 3 4 5 6	7 8 9 10 11 12 13 14 15	16 17 18 19 20 21 22 23	24 25 26 27 28 29 30 31	32 33 34 35 36 37 38 39	40 41 42 43 44 45 46 47 48 49	50 51 52 53 54	55 56 57 58 59 60 61 62 63 64 65 66	67 68 69 70 71 72 73 74 75 76	77 78	79 80
2 5 0 0			1 0	9	8				option	1 0 6
Reg. Pay $/Qtr.	Overtime ¢/Unit	Hiring Cost $/Person	High Price	Med. Price	Low Price	Sale Price $	Accumulated Depreciation	Area	Purchase Price $	Area	Capacity-Units	Co. No.
Prod. Worker Pay: Change to ($)			Material Cost: Change to ($)			Sale of Plant			Purchase of Plant			

© 1984 by Houghton Mifflin Company

TEMPOMATIC IV: A MANAGEMENT SIMULATION BY CHARLES R. SCOTT JR. AND ALONZO J. STRICKLAND III
COPYRIGHT HOUGHTON MIFFLIN, 1984 (RELEASE C1)

PAGE 1
QUARTER 7.

INDUSTRY 22.
TEAM 1

GIDGET COMPANY

PRODUCTION ANALYSIS
JULY 1 TO SEPTEMBER 30 YEAR 2.

MATERIAL	AREA 1 UNITS	$/UNIT	COST	AREA 2 UNITS	$/UNIT	COST	AREA 3 UNITS	$/UNIT	COST	TOTAL UNITS	COST
1. BEG. INV.	6000.	$6.48	$38838.	0.	$.00	$0.	0.	$.00	$0.	6000.	$38838.
2. RECEIPTS	10000.	$7.00	$70000.	0.	$.00	$0.	0.	$.00	$0.	10000.	$70000.
3. AVAILABLE	16000.	$6.81	$108838.	0.	$.00	$0.	0.	$.00	$0.	16000.	$108838.
4. USAGE	14400.	$6.81	$98026.	0.	$.00	$0.	0.	$.00	$0.	14400.	$98026.
5. FINAL INV.	1600.	$6.76	$10812.	0.	$.00	$0.	0.	$.00	$0.	1600.	$10812.
6. REC.-NEXT QTR	20000.	$8.00	$160000.	0.	$.00	$0.	0.	$.00	$0.	20000.	$160000.
7. AVAIL.-NEXT QT	21600.	$7.91	$170812.	0.	$.00	$0.	0.	$.00	$0.	21600.	$170812.

8. CARRY. COST ($ 1.00 X (1))   TOTAL COST $ 6000.
9. TOT. MAT. COST (4) + (8) $ 104026.

WORK FORCE

	THIS QUARTER AREA 1	AREA 2	AREA 3	TOTAL	NEXT QUARTER AREA 1	AREA 2	AREA 3	TOTAL
10. NO. WORKERS BEG. QTR.	41.	0.	0.	41.	55.	0.	0.	55.
11. WORKERS DISCHARGED	0.	0.	0.	0.				
12. WORKERS LOST TO T'OVER	3.	0.	0.	3.	2.	0.	0.	2.
13. WORKERS LAID OFF	0.	0.	0.	0.				
14. WORKERS AVAILABLE	38.	0.	0.	38.	53.	0.	0.	53.
15. CREWS AVAILABLE (CREW= 3)	12.	0.	0.	12.	17.	0.	0.	17.
16. WORKERS HIRED	17.	0.	0.	17.				
17. CREW PRODUCTIVITY	1000.	1000.	1000.	1000.	1000.	1000.	1000.	1000.
18. MAX. PROD. W/O O'TIME	12000.	0.	0.	12000.	17000.	0.	0.	17000.
19. PLANT CAP. AVAIL., UN.	13000.	0.	0.	13000.	18000.	0.	0.	18000.
20. PLANT UNDER CON., UN.	5000.	0.	0.		0.	0.	0.	
21. PLANT ORDERED, UNITS	0.	0.	0.					

MFG. COST OF GOODS SOLD

THIS QUARTER

		THIS QUARTER	TOTAL COST
1. MATERIAL			$ 104026.
2. LABOR-REG. PAY	($ 2500. X 55.)	$ 137500.	
3. LAYOFF COST	($ 0. X 0.)	0.	
4. OVER TIME PAY	($ 15.00 X 2400.)	36000.	
5. HIRING COST	($ 3000. X 17.)	51000.	
6. OVERHEAD	($224500. X 50%)		224500.
7. DEPRECIATION			112250.
			66000.

	UNITS	$/UNIT	TOTAL COST	NEXT QUARTER UNITS	$/UNITS	TOTAL COST
8. TOTAL MFG. COST	14400.	$ 35.19	$ 506776.			
9. BEG. FIN. GOODS INV.	721.	26.51	19116.			
10. TOTAL COST OF GOODS	15121.	34.78	525892.			
11. END FIN. GOODS INV.	743.	34.78	25841.	743.	$ 34.78	$ 25841.
12. MFG. COST OF GOODS SOLD	14378.	$ 34.78	$ 500051.			

GIDGET COMPANY

PAGE 2
QUARTER 7.
INDUSTRY 22.
TEAM 1

WAREHOUSE OPERATIONS
JULY 1 TO SEPTEMBER 30 YEAR 2.

| | THIS QUARTER | | | | NEXT QUARTER | | | |
	AREA 1	AREA 2	AREA 3	TOTAL	AREA 1	AREA 2	AREA 3	TOTAL
1. BEGINNING INVENTORY	719.	2.	0.	721.	743.	0.	0.	743.
2. UNITS ASSEMBLED	14400.	0.	0.	14400.				
3. UNITS AVAILABLE	15119.	2.	0.	15121.				
4. TRANSFER OF UNITS TO	0.	4500.	3000.	7500.				
5. TRANSFER OF UNITS FROM	7500.	0.	0.	7500.				
6. UNITS AVAILABLE FOR SALE	7619.	4502.	3000.	15121.				
7. UNITS SOLD	6876.	4502.	3000.	14378.				
8. ENDING INVENTORY	743.	0.	0.	743.				
9. UNITS OF SALES LOST	0.	336.	1.	743.				

WAREHOUSE AND FINISHED GOODS EXPENSE

10. COST OF UNITS TRANSFERRED		$ 30000.
11. COST OF CARRYING INVENTORY ($2.00 PER UNIT X 721.) $ 1442.	($2.00 PER UNIT X 743.)$ 1486.	
12. TOTAL COST OF WAREHOUSE OPERATIONS		31442.

SELLING AND ADMINISTRATIVE EXPENSE ANALYSIS

DESCRIPTION	AREA	1	2	3	TOTAL	RATE	EXPENSES	NEXT QTR. EXP.
1. SALES PERSONS HIRED (HIRING COST= $ 1100.)					2.	$ 4600.	$ 9200.	2.
2. SALES PERSONS IN TRAINING					0.	3500.	0.	10.
3. REGULAR SALES PERSONS		7.	3.	2.	12.	3500.	42000.	
4. TOTAL PERSONS IN SALES					14.	3657.	$ 51200.	
5. NATIONAL ADVERTISING (PAGES)					8.	3000.	24000.	$ 7000.
6. LOCAL ADVERTISING (PAGES)		8.	4.	3.	15.	900.	13500.	35000.
7. PRODUCT IMPROVEMENTS					0.	10000.	0.	
8. MARKET INFORMATION							8500.	
9. ADMINISTRATIVE EXPENSES							25000.	
10. TOTAL SELLING AND ADMINISTRATIVE EXPENSE							$ 122200.	

11. LOST SALES PERSONS (FOR NEXT QTR.)   2.

GIDGET COMPANY

CASH FLOW STATEMENT
JULY 1 TO SEPTEMBER 30 YEAR 2.

PAGE 3   INDUSTRY 22.
QUARTER 7.   TEAM 1

	THIS QTR.	NEXT QTR. (ESTIMATED)
CASH RECEIPTS		
1. CASH ON HAND BEGIN QTR.	$ 0.	$ 96998.
2. COLLECTION OF ACCOUNTS RECEIVABLE	600716.	542885.
3. STOCK, BOND, PLANT SALES INCOME	720000.	0.
4. TOTAL CASH AVAILABLE	$ 1320716.	$ 639883. (PLUS 10 PERCENT OF NEXT QUARTER'S SALES)
CASH PAYMENTS		
5. MATERIAL PURCHASES	$ 76000.	$ 161600.
6. NET SHORT TERM INTEREST	15098.	3081. (INTEREST RATE = 11.50 %)
7. INTEREST ON BONDS PAYABLE	14400.	12600.
8. DECLARED DIVIDENDS PAID	0.	0.
9. INCOME TAX PAID	15656.	0.
10. BOND AND STOCK RETIREMENT	80000.	80000.
11. PAYMENTS ON PLANT	400000.	0.
12. SHORT TERM LOAN + INVEST. PAYMENTS	132172.	107172.
13. LABOR + VARIABLE OVERHEAD	336750.	?
14. WAREHOUSE AND INVENTORY CARRY. COST	31442.	?
15. SELLING AND ADMINISTRATIVE EXPENSE	122200.	?
16. TOTAL CASH PAYMENTS	1223718.	364453. (PLUS DISCRETIONARY CASH PAYMENTS)
17. NET CASH BALANCE	$ 96998.	$ 275430.
18. SHORT TERM LOAN	0.	
19. CASH BALANCE AT END OF QTR.	$ 96998.	$ 275430. (BEFORE DISCRETIONARY CASH PAYMENTS)
20. ADDED INTEREST (INCLUDED IN LINE 6)		0.

GIDGET COMPANY

STATEMENT OF INCOME
JULY 1 TO SEPTEMBER 30 YEAR 2.

		THIS QUARTER		YEAR TO DATE
1.	NET SALES $40. $40. $40.	$	575120.	$	1773553.
2.	MANUFACTURING COST OF GOODS SOLD		500051.		1282732.
3.	SELLING AND ADMINISTRATIVE EXPENSES		122200.		354200.
4.	WAREHOUSE & INVENTORY CARRY. COSTS		31442.		103850.
5.	TOTAL OPERATING EXPENSES	$	653693.	$	1740782.
6.	OPERATING INCOME	$	-78573.	$	32771.
7.	NET INTEREST(EXPENSE LESS REVENUE)		29498.		75323.
8.	INCOME BEFORE INCOME TAXES	$	-108071.	$	-42552.
9.	PROVISION FOR INCOME TAXES (50 PERCENT)		0.		32758.
10.	NET INCOME AFTER TAXES	$	-108071.	$	-75310.
11.	DIVIDENDS DECLARED		0.		0.
12.	TO RETAINED EARNINGS	$	-108071.	$	-75310.
13.	NUMBER OF SHARES OUTSTANDING 160000.				
14.	EARNINGS PER SHARE	$	-.675	$	-.471
15.	DIVIDENDS PER SHARE	$	.000	$	.000

GIDGET COMPANY
STATEMENT OF FINANCIAL POSITION
SEPTEMBER 30 YEAR 2.

ASSETS

CURRENT ASSETS
1. CASH $ 96998.
2. ACCOUNTS RECEIVABLE   772933.
3. SHORT TERM INVESTMENTS   0.
   INVENTORIES
4.   RAW MATERIAL $ 10812.
5.   FINISHED GOODS   25841.   36653.
6.   TOTAL CURRENT ASSETS $ 906584.

INVESTMENTS
7. PLANTS AND EQUIPMENT AT COST $ 1820000.
8. LESS ACCUMULATED DEPRECIATION   412000.
9. NET PLANT   1408000.

10.   TOTAL ASSETS $ 2314584.

LIABILITIES
CURRENT LIABILITIES
11. NOTES PAYABLE $ 107172.
12. ESTIMATED INCOME TAX PAYABLE   0.
13. DIVIDENDS PAYABLE   0.
14.   TOTAL CURRENT LIABILITIES $ 107172.

LONG TERM DEBT
15. BONDS PAYABLE   #1   240000.
                          #2   320000.   560000.

16.   TOTAL LIABILITIES $ 667172.

STOCKHOLDERS' EQUITY

17. COMMON STOCK (PAR VALUE $10) $ 1600000.
18. ACCUM. RETAINED EARNINGS $ 155487.
19. ADD QUARTER EARNINGS   -108071.   47416.
20.   TOTAL STOCKHOLDERS' EQUITY   1647416.

21.   TOTAL LIABILITIES PLUS STOCKHOLDERS'EQUITY $ 2314588.

22. STOCKMARKET PRICE OF STOCK $ 8.67

DECISION SHEET for TEMPOMATIC IV (DO NOT PUNCH DECIMAL POINTS; PLACE LAST DIGIT OF EACH DECISION IN RIGHT COLUMN OF BOX)

CARD 1

| 1|2|3|4|5|6|7|8|9|10|11|12|13|14|15|16|17|18|19|20|21|22|23|24|25|26|27|28|29|30|31|32|33|34|35|36|37|38|39|40|41|42|43|44|45|46|47|48|49|50|51|52|53|54|55|56|57|58|59|60|61|62|63|64|65|66|67|68|69|70|71|72|73|74|75|76|77|78|79|80 |

| 1 | 1 | | | 9 | 4 | | 3 | | 2 | | 6 | | 2 | | 1 | | GIDGET | 2 2 | 5 1 |

Natl. Adv. No. Pgs. | Area 1 | Area 2 | Area 3 | Number of Salespersons | No. of Prod. Improvement | Area 1 | Area 2 | Area 3 | Company Name | Ind'y Number | Company Number + 50

Local Advertising-Number Pgs. | Sales Price Per Unit

CARD 2

| 1|2|3|4|5|6|7|8|9|10|11|12|13|14|15|16|17|18|19|20|21|22|23|24|25|26|27|28|29|30|31|32|33|34|35|36|37|38|39|40|41|42|43|44|45|46|47|48|49|50|51|52|53|54|55|56|57|58|59|60|61|62|63|64|65|66|67|68|69|70|71|72|73|74|75|76|77|78|79|80 |

| 8 | 1 | | 5000 | | 11000 | | 6000 | | 11000 | | GIDGET | 1 0 2 |

Quarter | Number of Salespersons Hired | Number of Salespersons Discharged | Area 1 | Area 2 | Area 3 | Total Trfd. | Area 1 | Area 2 | Area 3 | Company Name | Co. No.

Units Transferred To | Units Transferred From

CARD 3

| 1|2|3|4|5|6|7|8|9|10|11|12|13|14|15|16|17|18|19|20|21|22|23|24|25|26|27|28|29|30|31|32|33|34|35|36|37|38|39|40|41|42|43|44|45|46|47|48|49|50|51|52|53|54|55|56|57|58|59|60|61|62|63|64|65|66|67|68|69|70|71|72|73|74|75|76|77|78|79|80 |

| 20000 | | | | 150000 | | 40 | | 8500 | A B C D E F G H I | 1 0 3 |

Area 1 | Area 2 | Area 3 | Total S-T Loan Repayment-$ | % of Profit to Dividend | Dividend Per Share-¢ | Cost of Environment Information | Co. No.

Material Ordered-Units | Plant Ordered Constructed-Units | Environment Information

CARD 4

| 1|2|3|4|5|6|7|8|9|10|11|12|13|14|15|16|17|18|19|20|21|22|23|24|25|26|27|28|29|30|31|32|33|34|35|36|37|38|39|40|41|42|43|44|45|46|47|48|49|50|51|52|53|54|55|56|57|58|59|60|61|62|63|64|65|66|67|68|69|70|71|72|73|74|75|76|77|78|79|80 |

| 18000 | | | 3 | | | | | A1 A2 A3 | Cost | 1 0 4 |

Area 1 | Area 2 | Area 3 | Area 1 | Area 2 | Area 3 | Short-Term Investment | Deposit-$ | Withdraw-$ | Worker Layoffs | Co. No.

Total Actual Production-Units | Production Workers Hired-Number | Production Workers Discharged-Number

CARD 5

| 1|2|3|4|5|6|7|8|9|10|11|12|13|14|15|16|17|18|19|20|21|22|23|24|25|26|27|28|29|30|31|32|33|34|35|36|37|38|39|40|41|42|43|44|45|46|47|48|49|50|51|52|53|54|55|56|57|58|59|60|61|62|63|64|65|66|67|68|69|70|71|72|73|74|75|76|77|78|79|80 |

Number | Price | Amount $ | Interest-% per yr. X 100 | Amount of 1st Payment | Qtr. of 1st Pay. | Freq. of Pay. | Amount of Other Payment | Extra Pay-ment 1st Bond | Per Crew | Crew Size | Salary $/per. | Hiring $/per. | Co. No. | 1 0 5

Stock Issue-Share/¢ | Bonds: Issuance and Payment | Productivity | Salespersons

CARD 6

| 1|2|3|4|5|6|7|8|9|10|11|12|13|14|15|16|17|18|19|20|21|22|23|24|25|26|27|28|29|30|31|32|33|34|35|36|37|38|39|40|41|42|43|44|45|46|47|48|49|50|51|52|53|54|55|56|57|58|59|60|61|62|63|64|65|66|67|68|69|70|71|72|73|74|75|76|77|78|79|80 |

Reg. Pay $/Qtr. | Overtime ¢/Unit | Hiring Cost $/Person | Number | Med. Price | Low Price | High Price | Min. Price | Sale Price $ | Accumulated Depreciation | Area | Capacity-Units | Purchase Price $ | Area | Capacity-Units | Option | Co. No. | 1 0 6

Prod. Worker Pay: Change to ($) | Material Cost: Change to ($) | Stock Retired-Share/¢ | Sale of Plant | Purchase of Plant

© 1984 by Houghton Mifflin Company

TEMPOMATIC IV: A MANAGEMENT SIMULATION BY CHARLES R. SCOTT, JR. AND ALONZO J. STRICKLAND III
COPYRIGHT HOUGHTON MIFFLIN, 1984 (RELEASE C1)

PAGE 1 INDUSTRY 22.
QUARTER 8. TEAM 1

GIDGET COMPANY

PRODUCTION ANALYSIS
OCTOBER 1 TO DECEMBER 31 YEAR 2.

MATERIAL	AREA 1 UNITS	$/UNIT	COST	AREA 2 UNITS	$/UNIT	COST	AREA 3 UNITS	$/UNIT	COST	TOTAL UNITS	COST
1. BEG. INV.	1600.	$ 6.76	$ 10812.	0.	$ .00	$ 0.	0.	$ .00	$ 0.	1600.	10812.
2. RECEIPTS	20000.	$ 8.00	$ 160000.	0.	$ .00	$ 0.	0.	$ .00	$ 0.	20000.	160000.
3. AVAILABLE	21600.	$ 7.91	$ 170812.	0.	$ .00	$ 0.	0.	$ .00	$ 0.	21600.	170812.
4. USAGE	18000.	$ 7.91	$ 142433.	0.	$ .00	$ 0.	0.	$ .00	$ 0.	18000.	142433.
5. FINAL INV.	3600.	$ 7.88	$ 28379.	0.	$ .00	$ 0.	0.	$ .00	$ 0.	3600.	28379.
6. REC.-NEXT QTR	20000.	$ 8.00	$ 160000.	0.	$ .00	$ 0.	0.	$ .00	$ 0.	20000.	160000.
7. AVAIL.-NEXT QT	23600.	$ 7.98	$ 188379.	0.	$ .00	$ 0.	0.	$ .00	$ 0.	23600.	188379.

8. CARRY. COST ($ 1.00 X (1)) $ 1600.
9. TOT. MAT. COST (4) + (8) $ 144033.

WORK FORCE — THIS QUARTER

	AREA 1	AREA 2	AREA 3	TOTAL
10. NO. WORKERS BEG. QTR.	55.	0.	0.	55.
11. WORKERS DISCHARGED	0.	0.	0.	0.
12. WORKERS LOST TO T'OVER	2.	0.	0.	2.
13. WORKERS LAID OFF	0.	0.	0.	0.
14. WORKERS AVAILABLE	53.	0.	0.	53.
15. CREWS AVAILABLE(CREW = 3)	17.	0.	0.	17.
16. WORKERS HIRED	3.	0.	0.	3.
17. CREW PRODUCTIVITY	1000.	1000.	1000.	1000.
18. MAX. PROD. W/O O'TIME	17000.			17000.
19. PLANT CAP. AVAIL.,UN.	18000.			18000.
20. PLANT UNDER CON.,UN.	0.	0.	0.	0.
21. PLANT ORDERED,UNITS	0.	0.	0.	0.

WORK FORCE — NEXT QUARTER

	AREA 1	AREA 2	AREA 3	TOTAL
10.	56.	0.	0.	56.
12.	2.	0.	0.	2.
14.	54.	0.	0.	54.
15.	18.	0.	0.	18.
17.	1000.	1000.	1000.	1000.
18.	18000.			18000.
19.	18000.			18000.
20.	0	0	0	0

MFG. COST OF GOODS SOLD — THIS QUARTER

1. MATERIAL $ 140000.
2. LABOR—REG. PAY   ($ 2500. X   56.) $ 140000.
3.   LAYOFF COST ($ 0. X   0.)   0.
4.   OVER TIME PAY ($ 15.00 X 1000.)   15000.
5.   HIRING COST ($ 3000. X   3.)   9000.
6. OVERHEAD   ($164000. X 50%)
7. DEPRECIATION

	UNITS	$/UNIT	TOTAL COST
8. TOTAL MFG. COST	18000.	$ 26.72	$ 481033.
9. BEG. FIN. GOODS INV.	743.	34.78	25841.
10. TOTAL COST OF GOODS	18743.	27.04	506874.
11. END FIN. GOODS INV.	3189.	27.04	86241.
12. MFG. COST OF GOODS SOLD	15554.	$ 27.04	$ 420633.

NEXT QUARTER

	UNITS	$/UNITS	TOTAL COST
	26000	23.56	135000
	3189.	$ 27.04	$ 86241.
	23899	23.56	
	26388	23.56	

GIDGET COMPANY

WAREHOUSE OPERATIONS
OCTOBER 1 TO DECEMBER 31 YEAR 2.

PAGE 2
QUARTER 8.

INDUSTRY 22.
TEAM 1

	THIS QUARTER				NEXT QUARTER			
	AREA 1	AREA 2	AREA 3	TOTAL	AREA 1	AREA 2	AREA 3	TOTAL
1. BEGINNING INVENTORY	743.	0.	0.	743.	0.	1794.	1395.	3189.
2. UNITS ASSEMBLED	18000.	0.	0.	18000.				
3. UNITS AVAILABLE	18743.	0.	0.	18743.				
4. TRANSFER OF UNITS TO	0.	6000.	5000.	11000.				
5. TRANSFER OF UNITS FROM	11000.	0.	0.	11000.				
6. UNITS AVAILABLE FOR SALE	7743.	6000.	5000.	18743.				
7. UNITS SOLD	7743.	4206.	3605.	15554.				
8. ENDING INVENTORY	0.	1794.	1395.	3189.				
9. UNITS OF SALES LOST	28.	0.	0.	0.				

WAREHOUSE AND FINISHED GOODS EXPENSE

10. COST OF UNITS TRANSFERRED   ($2.00 PER UNIT X   743.) $ 44000.
11. COST OF CARRYING INVENTORY ($2.00 PER UNIT X   743.) $ 1486.   ($2.00 PER UNIT X   3189.)$
12. TOTAL COST OF WAREHOUSE OPERATIONS   45486.

SELLING AND ADMINISTRATIVE EXPENSE ANALYSIS

DESCRIPTION	AREA 1	2	3	TOTAL	RATE	EXPENSES	NEXT QTR. EXP.
1. SALES PERSONS HIRED (HIRING COST= $ 1100.)				1.	$ 4600.	$ 4600.	
2. SALES PERSONS IN TRAINING				2.	3500.	7000.	
3. REGULAR SALES PERSONS	6.	2.	2.	10.	3500.	35000.	
4. TOTAL PERSONS IN SALES				13.	3585.	$ 46600.	
5. NATIONAL ADVERTISING (PAGES)				11.	3000.	33000.	
6. LOCAL ADVERTISING (PAGES)	9.	4.	3.	16.	900.	14400.	
7. PRODUCT IMPROVEMENTS				1.	10000.	10000.	
8. MARKET INFORMATION						8500.	
9. ADMINISTRATIVE EXPENSES						25000.	
10. TOTAL SELLING AND ADMINISTRATIVE EXPENSE						$ 137500.	

11. LOST SALES PERSONS (FOR NEXT QTR.)   1.

© 1984 by Houghton Mifflin Company

GIDGET COMPANY

PAGE 3
QUARTER 8.

INDUSTRY 22.
TEAM 1

CASH FLOW STATEMENT
OCTOBER 1 TO DECEMBER 31 YEAR 2.

		THIS QTR.	NEXT QTR. (ESTIMATED)
	CASH RECEIPTS		
1.	CASH ON HAND BEGIN QTR.	$ 96998.	$ 58660.
2.	COLLECTION OF ACCOUNTS RECEIVABLE	605101.	541128.
3.	STOCK, BOND, PLANT SALES INCOME	0.	0.
4.	TOTAL CASH AVAILABLE	$ 702099.	$ 599788. (PLUS 10 PERCENT OF NEXT QUARTER'S SALES)
	CASH PAYMENTS		
5.	MATERIAL PURCHASES	$ 161600.	$ 163600.
6.	NET SHORT TERM INTEREST	3081.	3750. (INTEREST RATE = 10.00 %)
7.	INTEREST ON BONDS PAYABLE	12600.	10800.
8.	DECLARED DIVIDENDS PAID	0.	0.
9.	INCOME TAX PAID	0.	-52604.
10.	BOND AND STOCK RETIREMENT	80000.	80000.
11.	PAYMENTS ON PLANT	0.	0.
12.	SHORT TERM LOAN + INVEST. PAYMENTS	107172.	75000.
13.	LABOR + VARIABLE OVERHEAD	246000.	?
14.	WAREHOUSE AND INVENTORY CARRY. COST	45486.	?
15.	SELLING AND ADMINISTRATIVE EXPENSE	137500.	?
16.	TOTAL CASH PAYMENTS	793439.	280546. (PLUS DISCRETIONARY CASH PAYMENTS)
17.	NET CASH BALANCE	$ -91340.	$ 319242.
18.	SHORT TERM LOAN	150000.	
19.	CASH BALANCE AT END OF QTR.	$ 58660.	$ 319242. (BEFORE DISCRETIONARY CASH PAYMENTS)
20.	ADDED INTEREST (INCLUDED IN LINE 6)		0.

INDUSTRY 22.
TEAM 1

PAGE 4
QUARTER 8.

GIDGET COMPANY

STATEMENT OF INCOME
OCTOBER 1 TO DECEMBER 31 YEAR 2.

	THIS QUARTER	YEAR TO DATE
1. NET SALES $40. $40. $40.	$ 622160.	$ 2395713.
2. MANUFACTURING COST OF GOODS SOLD	420635.	1703365.
3. SELLING AND ADMINISTRATIVE EXPENSES	137500.	491700.
4. WAREHOUSE & INVENTORY CARRY. COSTS	45486.	149336.
5. TOTAL OPERATING EXPENSES	$ 603619.	$ 2344401.
6. OPERATING INCOME	$ 18541.	$ 51312.
7. NET INTEREST(EXPENSE LESS REVENUE)	15681.	91004.
8. INCOME BEFORE INCOME TAXES	$ 2860.	$ -39692.
9. PROVISION FOR INCOME TAXES (50 PERCENT)	-52604.C	-19845.
10. NET INCOME AFTER TAXES	$ 55464.	$ -19847.
11. DIVIDENDS DECLARED	0.	0.
12. TO RETAINED EARNINGS	$ 55464.	$ -19847.
13. NUMBER OF SHARES OUTSTANDING 160000.		
14. EARNINGS PER SHARE	$ .347	$ -.124
15. DIVIDENDS PER SHARE	$ .000	$ .000

C - TAX REFUND DUE TO LOSS CARRY BACK THIS YEAR AND/OR PREVIOUS YEAR

GIDGET COMPANY
STATEMENT OF FINANCIAL POSITION
DECEMBER 31 YEAR 2.

ASSETS

CURRENT ASSETS
1. CASH $ 58660.
2. ACCOUNTS RECEIVABLE   789992.
3. SHORT TERM INVESTMENTS   0.
   INVENTORIES
4.   RAW MATERIAL $ 28379.
5.   FINISHED GOODS   86241.   114620. $ 963272.
6.   TOTAL CURRENT ASSETS

INVESTMENTS
7. PLANTS AND EQUIPMENT AT COST $ 1820000.
8.   LESS ACCUMULATED DEPRECIATION   503000.
9. NET PLANT   1317000.

10.   TOTAL ASSETS $ 2280272.

LIABILITIES
CURRENT LIABILITIES
11. NOTES PAYABLE $ 150000.
12. ESTIMATED INCOME TAX PAYABLE   -52604.
13. DIVIDENDS PAYABLE   0.
14.   TOTAL CURRENT LIABILITIES $ 97396.

LONG TERM DEBT
15. BONDS PAYABLE   #1   200000.
                          #2   280000.   480000.

16.   TOTAL LIABILITIES $ 577396.

STOCKHOLDERS' EQUITY
17. COMMON STOCK (PAR VALUE $10) $ 1600000.
18. ACCUM. RETAINED EARNINGS $ 47416.
19. ADD QUARTER EARNINGS   55464.   102880.
20.   TOTAL STOCKHOLDERS' EQUITY   1702880.

21.   TOTAL LIABILITIES PLUS STOCKHOLDERS'EQUITY $ 2280276.

22. STOCKMARKET PRICE OF STOCK $ 9.76

Appendix C

Tempomatic Planning Model with VisiCalc

BY

PHILIP H. ANDERSON
College of St. Thomas
St. Paul, Minnesota

A. Introduction

The intent of this program is to allow you to ask a number of "what if" questions to aid your decision making process for the Tempomatic IV simulation. Remember, there is no guarantee that the actual results will equal those you have projected on the Tempomatic Planning Model (TPM). This will be dependent upon the accuracy of your estimate of sales of your product given the marketing tactics you have selected for that decision. The program is designed to give you insight into the impact of various decisions you might make without having to do a lot of number crunching.

The model described below is for using VisiCalc on an Apple computer. You can also use it on an IBM-PC or a TRS-80, but you will have to use different loading instructions (points 1–6), and a Tempo data disk that is compatible with the type of computer you are using. These will be provided by your instructor. The remaining instructions (points 7–21) will stay the same.

It is suggested that rather than doing all your analysis on the microcomputer, use it to generate the results given the worse possible scenario as a consequence of your decision. Then have it generate results for the best possible scenario, plus two in between. Use these results as management tools to make your final decision. REMEMBER, this program is *only* to serve as an *aid* for you to make your decisions. It will not make the decisions for you, the TPM results will *not* cause the Tempomatic IV results to equal your desired results. It is only a modeling tool.

B. Working with Diskettes

Be very careful when working with your diskettes. Each disk (or diskette) is magnetically coated and sealed in a protective cover. Do not touch the exposed magnetic surface. Protect it by keeping it in the paper sleeve when not in use. Keep it away from TVs or other devices that generate a magnetic field. Do not expose it to extremes in temperature (i.e., the inside of a car on a hot day) or write on the cover with a hard pen or pencil. A soft felt tip pen can be used lightly. When inserting the disk into the disk drive, insert it label side up, label in last, then close the drive door.

C. The VisiCalc Screen*

After you have loaded the VisiCalc program (discussed below), your screen will look like the photo below.

*From VisiCalc Users Guide, pp. 2-1 to 2-2, VISICORP, Inc.

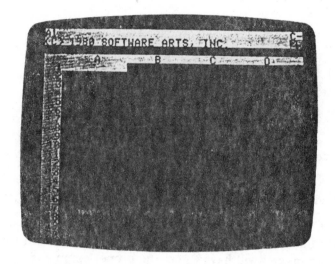

Your screen has become a **window** into the computer's memory. The VisiCalc program has organized the screen as an **electronic worksheet** by dividing it into rows and columns. Rows are vertically numbered (1, 2, 3, etc.) while columns are horizontally lettered (A, B, C, etc.). Each intersection of a row and a column **coordinate** (A1, B3, C17) marks an **entry position.**

At each entry position, you can type in a message, a number, or formula. In a moment, we'll demonstrate how you can write at different entry positions on this electronic worksheet.

Look at the white bar and dark line at the top of the screen (just above the column labels). This is called the **status area.** The bar is actually two lines. The top line is called the **entry line** and the second line is the **prompt line.** The prompt line currently displays the VisiCalc copyright notice and **version number.** Normally it will remain blank, except when you are entering commands such as the loading and saving of files (discussed later). It will then "prompt" you on what entries to make.

The dark line below the prompt line is called the **edit line.** When you are in the process of typing in an entry, but before you press the RETURN key, your entry will show up on the Edit line. After you press the RETURN key, your entry will move from the Edit line to the Entry line.

The right corner of the status area includes:
- a) The **Recalculation Order Indicator** (to be discussed under point #9 below). It will be either a "C" or an "R." The example above shows a "C."
- b) the **Memory Indicator** that tells how much memory is available (the number may be different on your computer). The example above shows a 25.
- c) the **Direction Indicator** which will be discussed under point #8 below. The direction indicator is the line (either horizontal or vertical) located just after the Recalculation Order Indicator.

D. Procedure for Using the Tempomatic Planning Model

You have to use two "floppy disks" when working with TPM. One is VISICALC, which is used to format the program. It simply creates a matrix within which the formulas on the second disk operate. To operate TPM use the following steps:

1. Turn on the printer, keyboard, and screen. The switch for the printer is in the back on the left. Locations for the printer and screen will vary with the equipment used. Ask for assistance if necessary.

If, when you turn on the keyboard, you hear a whir in the disk drive and the red "IN USE" light comes on, you have an Autostart system. Proceed directly to point #2. If you do not have an Autostart system, the disk drive will remain inactive. To start this type of system, you must perform the following steps.

    a. Press the RESET key.
    b. Type in 6.
    c. Hold down the CTRL key while pressing P
    d. Press the RETURN key.

Now proceed to point #2.

2. Press the RESET key on the keyboard. A character that looks like "]" will appear on the screen. If it doesn't you may have to hold down the CTRL key while pressing the RESET key.

3. Type in PR#1 and press the RETURN key. This turns on the printer.

4. Type in PRINT CHR$(29) and press the RETURN key. This will condense the printing so it will fit on an 80 column printer for most printers. If this does not result in condensed printing, you will have to get the proper command from your computer center consultant. If you should be working with a 100 column printer this step would be optional.

5. Type in PR#6, put the VISICALC disk in the first disk drive, close the drive door, and press the RETURN key. A small red light on the disk drive will light up to let you know the disk is being "loaded" (i.e., read) into the Apple's memory. Computerese for this is called "booting" or "booting the disk." When the light goes out, it is done loading the VISICALC disk and it is ready for the TEMPO disk.

   DO NOT ever try to remove a disk while the red light is on. This is a signal that the disk drive is in operation. You will most likely destroy the disk if you try to remove it while the disk drive is operating.

6. Remove the VISICALC disk and insert the TEMPO disk. Type in /SL TEMPO3 and press the RETURN key. The red light will come on again while the TEMPO program is being loaded. It will take a moment or two for the loading process to be completed. If you look at the top of your screen, the prompt line will indicate that the loading process is occurring. The memory indicator will change, decreasing in amount, as memory is used to load the program.

7. On the screen there will appear the first part of a matrix that extends from "A" to "N" across the top and from "1" to "240" downward. Actually VISICALC creates a matrix larger than this, but that is the extent of the matrix that TEMPO uses. An example of what your output will look like is included in Exhibit #1. Included on the example are the matrix labels (A, B, C, etc., and 1, 2, 3, etc.) to aid in your identification of position locations of the entries in the matrix. Note that the screen is not capable of showing the whole TPM matrix, just a segment of it.

8. To move around the matrix you move the cursor (a white bar on the screen). Its initial location will be in position A1. To move it left or right, press the arrows "←" or "→" in the lower right corner of the keyboard. To move up or down, press the space bar then the left arrow "←" to move up or the right arrow "→" to move down. To return to a left or right movement, press the space bar and then the arrow pointing the direction you want to move. To know whether the cursor will move horizontally or vertically, look at the direction indicator in the upper right corner.

9. Before you begin entering data into the model, press the shift key and then the exclamation point (!) while continuing to hold down the shift key. This will initialize (i.e., set up) the program by causing it to calculate the formulas presently in the matrix. Without doing this, many of the cell locations would show "ERROR" on the screen. This is because their value is determined by the value of another cell and until a calculation is performed a value has yet to be determined for these cells. It may be necessary to repeat this step to eliminate all the error messages that might occur. This is normal and does not mean you have a problem with your program. Whenever you wish to make an "upper case" entry (e.g., an exclamation point), use the shift key like you would on a typewriter, holding it down while typing in the desired character.

Note: Notice in the upper right hand corner there will be either an R or a C on the screen. This tells you the order of recalculation that will be performed on the entries you make to the model. An "R" indicates that the VisiCalc program is recalculating by rows, starting with Row 1 (i.e., A1 to N1) and proceeding downward. A "C" indicates it is recalculating by columns, starting with Column 1 (i.e., A1 to A240) and proceeding to the right. It is best to calculate by rows when using this model. If there is a C in the upper right hand corner, type /GOR and an R should appear.

If the VisiCalc program appears to have calculated the formulas incorrectly, it is probably because it made its calculations based on formulas that were calculated out of the proper sequence. To correct this just press the shift key and the exclamation point once or twice, until the numbers you are evaluating stop changing.

10. You are now ready to begin entering the data of *your* choosing into the model. Begin by entering the quarter number that you will be modeling (position B1 on your matrix). To make this entry, move the cursor to position B1, type in the quarter number (e.g., 9), and press the RETURN key. The cursor will disappear while the entry is being made in the program and will reappear after it has completed the entry. The order of recalculation indicator will also flash off and on while the recalculation is occurring and will stop after it has completed the entry. Although not the case with this entry, several numbers will change if they are related to the number you are changing. Next enter the Beginning Inventory Units (B7) and the Beginning Inventory Cost (D7) for the quarter you are modeling. These will be the same as the Final Inventory figures for the quarter preceding the one you are modeling. For Quarter 9 the Beginning Inventory figures will be 3600 (units) and 28379 (cost) as taken from your Quarter 8 output in your Tempomatic IV manual. $/unit will be calculated automatically.

Note that there may be some slight differences in the cost figures for your TPM model and those generated by the mainframe computer's output. This is because of differences between the two regarding the number of decimal places that are carried when determining average prices per unit. These differences will not materially affect the results that are generated by the TPM model. Remember, the TPM model is not used to predict precisely what will actually happen on your next decision. Rather, it is to provide you with information on the basic consequences of possible decisions you might make!

11. Complete the **Materials** section of the matrix by making material entries, where necessary, for Receipts Units (B8) and Receipts $/Units (C8), Usage Units (B10), and Received Next Quarter (B12 and C12). Note that in some cases you will have to enter material per unit prices, but in most cases they will be calculated for you. Also, if you build plants in areas 2 or 3 you will have to make corresponding entries in those areas as well.

Note: If there is a question in your mind about whether it is all right to make an entry in a particular position, check the upper left corner of the screen. If there is an (L) it means that the space on the matrix has been programmed to have a label in it. Following the "L" will be the label (e.g., "COST"). Do not make an entry here! If there is a (V) it means that the space has been programmed to have a value in it. This can either be a number (e.g., 300) or a formula (e.g., B7*C7, which means to multiply the number in B7 by the number in C7 and enter the result in this position). **If there is a *formula* after the (V), DO NOT MAKE AN ENTRY!!** If you type in a number, it will eliminate the formula and replace it with whatever number you have typed in. Be careful and remember the letter "O" looks exactly like a zero except that a zero has a slash (i.e., "/") through it and looks like "∅". As a result, "(V) 071" may look like a number but it is really a formula. Be cautious. If you should accidentally eliminate a formula, you will have to go back to point #6 and reload the Tempo disk.

12. Once you have completed the **Material** section of the matrix (A6 through L16), move on to the **Workforce** section (A18 through K31). Make the necessary changes for this quarter for the number of workers beginning the quarter (C19), any workers discharged (C20), the workers lost to turnover (C21), the number of workers laid off (C22), and the number of workers hired (C26). If you have added plant in other areas, the appropriate entries must be made. If you have ordered construction of *new* plant capacity, make the appropriate entry on line 31 (D31 and/or E31). If you have purchased *used* plant facilities, make the appropriate entry on line 30 (D30 and/or E30). The changes for Next Quarter (H18 through K30) should occur automatically.

    Changes in crew size or crew productivity will be discussed later under the section "Making Changes in Simulation Variables."

13. Next, move to the **Sales Estimate** section (H35-K46) and make entries for the Unit Sales you are targeting to achieve (I41, I43, I45) and the Sales Prices (J41, J43, J45) you estimate will yield your desired sales volume. Total Unit Sales (I47), Average Sales Price (J47), and Total Dollar Sales (K47) will be calculated automatically.

14. Just below the **Sales Estimate** section is the **Accounts Receivable Calculation** section (I51-K63). The entry for Quarter "X" sales (i.e., this quarter's sales) is automatically calculated based on your sales estimate above. Entries must be made for the two preceding quarters' sales. For example, if you are working on estimating Quarter 9 sales (Qtr "X"), you must enter the actual sales for Quarter 8 (Qtr "X-1") and Quarter 7 (Qtr "X-2") in positions K56 and K57, respectively. The total receipts for the quarter you are estimating will be calculated automatically.

15. Most of the **Mfg. Cost of Goods Sold** section (A35-E52) is automatically calculated. If you have added plant capacity you will have to change the depreciation cost (E44). An entry must be made to update the Beginning Finished Goods Inventory (C48) and its total cost (E48). This entry comes from the ending finished goods inventory for the *preceding* quarter (pg. 1, line 11, Mfg. Cost of Goods Sold Section of your computer printout). For Quarter 9, you would use the Quarter 8 figures, 3189 units at a total cost of $86,241. No other entries are needed in this section. The Ending Finished Goods Inventory (C50-E50) and Mfg. Cost of Goods Sold (C52-E52) will be automatically calculated based on your Units Sold (I47) decision in the Sales Estimate section.

16. The **Warehouse Operations** section (A55-F65) needs entries for Beginning Inventory (C58-E58), Units Transferred to (C61-E61) and Units Transferred From (C62-E62). Beginning Inventory for Quarter 9 will be your ending inventory for Quarter 8. The other entries are at your discretion, made to achieve the ending inventory you

desire. Units Sold (C64-E64) will be carried down from your estimates above. The **Warehouse and Finished Goods Expense** section (A70-D76) will be calculated automatically.

17. The **Selling and Administrative Expense** section (A79-H95) requires entries for Sales Reps Hired (F84), Sales Reps in Training (F85), Regular Sales Reps (C86-E86), National Ads (F89), Local Ads (C90-E90), Product Improvements (F91), and Market Information (H92). If you add plant capacity in other areas you will have to change the Administrative Expense (H93).

18. The **Cash Flow** section (A100-G130) requires entries for Cash on Hand (D105), cash received *if* there were any stock, bond, or plant sales (D107), and material purchases (D113) *through* short term loans and investment payments (C120). These can be taken from those entries under Next Quarter on the Cash Flow Statement of your latest output. (The only exception to this is if you make a short term investment this quarter, that amount must be added to the Short Term Loan and Investment Payment figure.) Exhibit #1 shows entries made for Quarter 9, based on Quarter 8 output. Costs for Labor and Variable Overhead (D121), Warehouse Expenses (D122), and Selling and Administrative Expenses (D123) will be entered automatically from earlier calculations. Next you must determine the short term loan amount you wish to request (D128).

Note that there is a column for estimating cash flow for your next quarter as well. Most of these entries are simple extensions of the current quarter's costs so that you can get some sense of the impact on cash flow if there are no significant changes to present operations.

19. All entries for the **Balance Sheet and Income Statement** are located in the Balance Sheet and Income Calculations section (H136-L157). The first eight entries are made based on figures from your last quarter's output. Plant and Equipment At Cost (L142) will remain the same unless you change your plant size. Note that Accumulated Retained Earnings is the sum of past accumulated earnings (47416 in Qtr 8) plus earnings from the addition of the most recent quarter's earnings (55464 in Qtr 8). Therefore, when working on Quarter 9 the figure from Quarter 8 is 102,880. The payments on the bonds (L146 and L148) will remain the same unless a new bond is taken out or a bond is paid off, at which time an entry of zero must be made.

The last three entries are made based on decisions you have made for this quarter. Enter any short-term investments you made in L155. If you pay dividends, enter the per share amount in L156. Also, if you elect to issue or retire shares of stock, you will have to change the number of shares outstanding (L157).

Based on these and earlier entries an Income Statement and a "rough" Balance Sheet are constructed. Do not expect an exact balancing of Assets with Liabilities and Stockholders' Equity. Its purpose is to give you an idea of the impact of your decisions on your Balance Sheet.

Also, the TPM VisiCalc model is not capable of maintaining a provision for income taxes that will allow for loss carry forwards, etc. The model simply calculates tax obligations at 50 percent of income before tax. This tax obligation will be reflected in income tax to be paid *next quarter* on the Cash Flow Statement, the provision for taxes on the Income Statement, and the income taxes payable on the Balance Sheet. If you have a tax credit due your company, you will have to calculate this manually to determine your total net income.

20.   The **Analysis Section** (C218-C239) includes some calculations which are automatically made based on prior entries. No entries are made in this section.

21.   In order to print out a copy of the above information, return the cursor to location A1. Type in /P1 and press RETURN. Notice the prompt line is asking for the lower right corner position location for the matrix you want to print out. Next type in N240 (which is the lower right hand corner of the matrix you are working on) and press RETURN. This should begin the printing process. Once printing has been completed the cursor will automatically return to position A1. If you wish to make some changes to your prior decision set that was just printed out (such as sales prices or sales volume), return to Step #9 and continue on from there through Step #20. **Note that you only have to make entries where you wish to make changes.** For example, if the only changes you want to make are sales prices and units sold, simply go to the Sales Estimate section and make the appropriate changes. The program retains the latest entries you have made until you turn the computer off. Therefore, do not turn off the computer until *after* you have tested all the alternative scenarios you plan to consider and you have saved your latest file (see discussion below on saving files).

Also, if you don't want the entire model printed, simply position the cursor in what would be the upper left corner of the section you want printed, type /P1, press RETURN, then type the lower right corner where you want printing to stop. For example, if all you wanted to print was the Warehouse operations section, put the cursor in position A55, press RETURN, type F65, and press RETURN.

E. Saving Files

If you are finished making the entries you wish to make, you can save the latest set of data on your worksheet for future use. That is, rather than always starting with the Quarter 9 figures as shown in Exhibit #1, *you can build off of figures from* the quarter prior to the one you will be working on by saving that prior quarter's data. That is, you can use your Quarter 10 figures as the basis for working on Quarter 11. This is done by using the /S command.

When you type /S (the VisiCalc storage command) the prompt line should read as shown below:

STORAGE: L   S   D   I   Q   #

The VisiCalc program is telling you that it has recognized /S as the Storage command and that it expects you to choose from one of six forms of the storage command by pressing one of these keys: L S D I Q #. These keys are command symbols for the following:

L   Load the worksheet contents into its memory from a diskette file
S   Save the sheet in memory by "writing" it into a diskette file
D   Delete a previously saved file from its place on the diskette
I   Initialize, or format, a blank diskette. **Do not type this as it will completely erase whatever is on your disk.**
save or load a worksheet in the DATA INTERCHANGE FORMAT

Press the letter S and STORAGE: FILE FOR SAVING will appear on the prompt line with the edit cue on the edit line. Because each diskette has enough room to hold several electronic worksheets, each worksheet on the same diskette must have a unique name. In this way you can find the worksheet at a later time and load it back into the computer. Do not use TEMPO3 for your file name. You should always be able to access TEMPO3 for the model of Quarter 8 decisions. Use your company name in the Tempomatic game for your TPM file name. Save a final copy each quarter, distinguishing it by the quarter number in this manner:

Gidget12

Gidget13

Gidget14, etc.

When you want to recall a stored file, type /SL and then the file name you wish to load (i.e., recall) from your diskette.

If you should try to save more files than what your diskette can hold, you will have to choose some files to delete to make room for the current ones you want to save. To do this, type /SD, the file name you wish to delete, then press RETURN. Since this action will completely erase a file from storage on the disk, the prompt line will ask you to type Y to confirm that this is what you want to do. Typing Y will complete the deleting process. Typing any other key will cancel the command.

Return the cursor to position A1 before initiating the file saving process. Although not necessary, the cursor always starts (after loading) in the same position it was in when the file was saved. By having it in position A1 when you save the file, you will always be at the beginning of your model after loading it for your next decision.

F. Additional Commands for Working with VISICALC

1. Rather than having to press one of the arrows multiple times to move to a distant position on the matrix from where you are, use the "GO TO" command. Press the > key (this will require holding down the SHIFT key while pressing the > key). Next, type in the location on the matrix you wish to go to; e.g., I35. Press RETURN and the cursor will automatically move to position I35.

2. At times you may wish to monitor two distant sections of the matrix at the same time. This can be done by splitting the screen. Move to the section highest in the matrix that you wish to work with (e.g., the Sales Estimate section), then move the cursor to the middle of the screen. Type /WH and the screen will be split horizontally. To move from one half of the screen to the other, press the semicolon (;). You move around each half of the screen like you would on the full screen. To return to the full screen, type /W1.

   For example, position the Sales Estimate Section on the top half of the screen. Next position the cursor just under the Average Sales Price figure shown (i.e., coordinate J47). Type /WH and the screen will be split horizontally. Press the semicolon (;) and the cursor will move to the lower half of the screen. Type >A218, press RETURN and the bottom half of the screen will show the Analysis Section. Press the semicolon to return to the Sales Estimate Section in the top half of the screen. Now you can select various prices for your product and simultaneously see the impact this has on breakeven, return on sales, etc.

3. If at any time you want to "get out of" a command or entry you have *typed in* but not yet "entered" by pressing the RETURN key, type CTRL C by *holding down* the CTRL key *while* pressing C. This allows you to "escape" from any entry you have not completed or entered. If there is just a minor change that you want to make, typing the ESC key will cause the edit cue to back up, erasing the letter or number to its immediate left. If you type the ESC key often enough, you can "back out" of the entry you are making. That is, if you keep backing up and erase all the elements of the entry you have made, you will accomplish the same thing as if you had typed CTRL C.

4. **NEVER press the RESET key unless you want to return your Apple II to a startup condition.** The RESET key will interrupt the normal program operation and erase *everything* you have entered, requiring you to reload the VisiCalc program.

5. The REPT key (i.e., Repeat KEY) allows you to move around the worksheet more rapidly. Instead of typing one of the arrows (← or →) multiple times to move the cursor, just hold the REPT key and the desired arrow down at the same time. This provides a means for moving around the worksheet quickly, although not as quickly as the "GO TO" command discussed above.

G. Making Changes in Simulation Variables

There are likely to be times where you will have to make changes in the costs of various elements in your model (i.e., inventory carrying costs) to match changes made by the Tempomatic simulation administrator. To make these changes, go to the position location given in the table below for the element you want to change and enter the new cost figure as you would any other entry.

Table #1

Element	Position
Carrying Costs (Raw Materials)	F14
Carrying Costs (Finished Goods)	C73
Transfer Costs	C72
Crew Size	C24 & H24
Crew Productivity	C27 & H27
Pay Rate for Production Workers	C39
Layoff Costs	C40
Overtime Rate	C41
Hiring Costs for Production Workers	C42
Overhead Rate	C43
Hiring Costs for Sales Representatives	E83
Pay Rate for Sales Reps	G84 & G85
National Advertising Costs/Page	G88
Local Advertising Costs/Page	G89
Cost of Product Improvements	G90

H. VisiCalc vs. the Tempomatic Planning Model

The Tempomatic Planning Model only scratches the surface of what VisiCalc can do and how you can work with it. Hopefully it has served to show you the power of working with financial spread sheet programs like VisiCalc and whetted your appetite to learn more. There are many books printed which discuss VisiCalc in more detail. Hopefully, you are encouraged to "take the plunge" and learn more about this popular software.

TEMPOMATIC PLANNING MODEL
SHORT FORM

1. Turn on printer, keyboard, and screen.

2. Press: RESET

3. Type: PR#1
   Press: RETURN

4. Type: PRINT CHR$(29) or the appropriate command for condensed printing.
   Press: RETURN

5. Type: PR#6
    Insert: VISICALC disk in DISK DRIVE #1
    Press: RETURN

6. Remove: VISICALC disk
    Insert: TEMPO disk
    Type: /SL TEMPO3
    Press: RETURN

7, 8, & 9. No Entry

10. Enter: Beginning Inventory (B7)
    Cost   (D7)
    plus: similar entries for Areas 2 & 3 if needed

11. Enter: if needed: Receipts, Units & $/Units (B8) & (C8)
                       Usage Units   (B10)
                       Receipts Next Qtr   (B12) & (C12)

12. Enter: No. Workers Beginning Qtr (C19)
    Workers Discharged   (C20)
    Turnover   (C21)
    Workers Laid Off   (C22)
    Workers Hired   (C26)

13. Enter: Projected Unit Sales (I41, I43, I45)
    Sales Price   (J41, J43, J45)

14. Enter: Qtr "X-1" Sales   (K56)
    Qtr "X-2" Sales   (K57)

15. Enter: Depreciation   (E44)
    Beg. Finished Goods Inv. (C48)
    B.F.G.I. Cost   (E48)

16. Enter: Beg. Finished Goods Inv. (C58-E58)
    Units Transferred To   (C61-E61)
    Units Transferred From (C62-E62)

17. Enter: Sales Reps Hired   (F84)
    Sales Reps in Training   (F85)
    Regular Sales Reps   (C86-E86)
    National Ads   (F89)
    Local Ads   (C90-E90)
    Product Improvements   (F91)
    Market Information   (F92)

18. Enter: Cash on Hand   (D105)
    Stock, Bond, Plant Sales   (D107), if necessary
    Material Purchases   (D113)
    Net Short Term Interest   (D114)
    Bond Interest   (D115)
    Dividends Paid   (D116)
    Income Tax Paid   (D117)
    Bond & Stock Retirement   (D118)
    Payments on Plant   (D119)
    Short-Term Loan & Investment Payment (D120)
    Short-Term Loan Requested   (D128)

19. Enter: Plant and Equipment   (L142)
    Accumulated Depreciation   (L143)
    Notes Payable   (L144)

Accumulated Retained Earnings   (L145)
Bond #1   (L146)
Payment on Bond #1   (L147)
Bond #2   (L148)
Paymend on Bond #2   (L149)
Short Term Investment   (L155)
Dividend Payments/Share   (L156)
Shares Outstanding   (L157)

20. No Entries Required

21. Return cursor to position A1

    Type: /P1
    Press: RETURN
    Type: N240
    Press: RETURN

EXHIBIT #1

1 QUARTER # 9   TEMPO

PRODUCTION ANALYSIS
****

		AREA 1			AREA 2			AREA 3			TOTAL	
6	MATERIAL	UNITS	$/UNIT	COST	UNITS	$/UNIT	COST	UNITS	$/UNIT	COST	UNITS	COST
7	BEG. INV.	3600	7.88	28379	0	0.00	0	0	0.00	0	3600	28379
8	RECEIPTS	20000	8.00	160000	0	0.00	0	0	0.00	0	20000	160000
9	AVAIL	23600	7.98	188379	0	0.00	0	0	0.00	0	23600	188379
10	USAGE	19000	7.98	151661	0	0.00	0	0	0.00	0	19000	151661
11	FIN INV	4600	7.98	36718	0	0.00	0	0	0.00	0	4600	36718
12	REC NQTR	20000	8.00	160000	0	0.00	0	0	0.00	0	20000	160000
13	AVL NQTR	24600	8.00	196718	0	0.00	0	0	0.00	0	24600	196718

14   CARRYING COSTS = BEGINNING INV. UNITS X $ 1   3600
                                                                ——————

16 TOTAL MATERIAL COSTS   155261

		THIS QUARTER				NEXT QUARTER			
18	WORK FORCE	AREA 1	AREA 2	AREA 3	TOTAL	AREA 1	AREA 2	AREA 3	TOTAL
19	NO. WKRS BEG. QTR	56	0	0	56	56	0	0	56
20	WKRS DISCHARGED	0	0	0	0				
21	WKR TURNOVER	2	0	0	2	2	0	0	2
22	WKRS LAID OFF	0	0	0	0				
23	WKRS AVAILABLE	54	0	0	54	54	0	0	54
24	CREW SIZE	3	3	3		3	3	3	
25	CRWS AVAILABLE	18	0	0	18	18	0	0	18
26	WKRS HIRED	2	0	0	2				
27	CREW PRODUCTIVITY	1000	1000	1000	1000	1000	1000	1000	1000
28	MAX PROD. W/O OT	18000	0	0	18000	18000	0	0	18000
29	PLNT CAP AVL.UNTS	18000	0	0	18000	18000	0	0	18000
30	PLNT UND CNSTR UN	0	0	0	0	0	0	0	0
31	PLNT ORD, UNITS	0	0	0	0				

```
35              MFG. COST OF GOODS SOLD
                ****************************
                            RATE    COST     TOTAL
38    MATERIAL                              155261
39    LABOR-REG. PAY =      2500   140000
40          LAYOFF COST        0        0
41        OVR.TIME PAY        15    15000
42        HIRING COST      3000     6000   161000
43    OVERHEAD (%)          0.50             80500
44    DEPRECIATION                           91000
45
46                         UNITS  $/UNIT TOT COST
47    TOTAL MFG COST       19000   25.67   487761
48    BEG. FIN.GOODS INV    3189   27.04    86241
49    TOTAL CST OF GOODS   22189   25.87   574002
50    END.FIN. GOODS INV    5339   25.87   138113
51
52    MFG.COST GOODS SLD   16850   25.87   435889


55                    WAREHOUSE OPERATIONS
56                    *********************
57                    AREA 1   AREA 2   AREA 3   TOTAL
58    BEG. INVENTORY        0     1794     1395    3189
59    UNITS ASSEMBLED   19000        0        0   19000
60    UNITS AVAILABLE   19000     1794     1395   22189
61    TRNSF UNITS TO        0     4800     4500    9300
62    TRNSF UNITS FROM   9300        0        0    9300
63    UNITS AVL FOR SALE 9700     6594     5895   22189
64    UNITS SOLD         8500     4500     3850   16850
65    ENDING INVENTORY   1200     2094     2045    5339


70    WAREHOUSE AND FINISHED GOODS EXPENSE
      *************************************
72                      $/UNIT    COST
73    COST OF UNS TRNSF=  4.00    37200
74    COST TO CARRY INV=  2.00     6378
                                  ------
76    TOTAL COST OF WHSE           43578
```

```
******************************************************
*                 SALES ESTIMATES                    *
*                 ---------------                     *
*                PROJECTED  SALES   PROJECTED         *
*   AREA           UNITS    PRICE     SALES           *
*   ----         ---------  -----   -------           *
*                                                     *
*   AREA 1         8500      40     340000            *
*                                                     *
*   AREA 2         4500      40     180000            *
*                                                     *
*   AREA 3         3850      40     154000            *
*                                                     *
*   TOTAL         16850     40.00   674000            *
*                                                     *
******************************************************
     *                                    *
     *    ACCOUNTS RECEIVABLE             *
     *       CALCULATION                  *
     *                                    *
     *                                    *
     *   QTR "X" SALES          674000    *
     *   QTR "X-1" SALES        622160    *
     *   QTR "X-2" SALES        575120    *
     *                                    *
     *   RECEIPTS                         *
     *     THIS QTR            67400      *
     *     PAST QTRS          541128      *
     *                        ------      *
     *     TOTAL             608528       *
     *                                    *
     **************************************
```

```
79              SELLING AND ADMINISTRATIVE EXPENSE
                **********************************

82    DESCRIPTION        AREA 1  AREA 2  AREA 3  TOTAL  RATE   EXPENSES
83    -----------        ------  ------  ------  -----  ----   --------
84    SALES REPS HIRED: HIRING COSTS = $ 1100      2    4600     9200
85    SALES REPS IN TRNG                           1    3500     3500
86    REG SALES REPS       7       2       3      12    3500    42000
87      TOTAL SALES REPS                          15    3647    54700
```

89	NATIONAL ADVERTISING				10	3000	30000
90	LOCAL ADVERTISING	11	5	5	21	900	18900
91	PRODUCT IMPROVEMENTS				2	10000	20000
92	MARKET INFORMATION						3000
93	ADMINISTRATIVE EXP						25000

95	TOTAL SELL&ADM.EXPENSE						151600

CASH FLOW STATEMENT
****

	CASH RECEIPTS	THIS QTR.	NEXT QTR.		
	-------------	---------	---------		
105	CASH ON HAND	58660	24964		
106	COLLECTION OF ACCR	608528	608528		
107	STK,BND,PLANT SALE	0	0		
108	TOTAL CASH AVL.		667188		633492

	CASH PAYMENTS				

113	MATERIAL PURCHASES	163600	164600		
114	NET SHRT TRM INT	3750	3750		
115	INT ON BNDS PAY	10800	10800		
116	DECLARED DIV.PAID	0	0		
117	INC.TAX PAID	-52604	14192		
118	BND&STK RETIREMENT	80000	80000		
119	PAYMENTS ON PLANT	0	0		
120	SHRT TRM LN&INV.PM	75000	112500		
121	LABOR&VAR.OVERHEAD	241500	241500		
122	WAREHSE&INV.CR CST	43578	43578		
123	SELL&ADM EXPENSES	151600	151600		
124	TOTAL CASH PYMT		717224		822520
126	NET CASH BALANCE	-50036	-189028		
128	SHRT TRM LOAN REQUESTED	75000	75000		
130	CASH BAL.END QTR.		24964		-114028

```
136                 STATEMENT OF INCOME
                    *******************
                                        THIS QTR.
139   NET SALES                           674000
140   MFG.COST OF GOODS SOLD              435889

142   GROSS PROFIT                        238111
143
144   SELL&ADM EXPENSE                    151600
145   WAREHOUSE EXPENSE                    43578
146
147   OPERATING INCOME                     42933
148
149   NET INTEREST(EXP-REV)                14550

151   INCOME BEFORE TAX                    28383

153   PROVISION FOR TAXES                  14192

155   NET INCOME AFTER TAXES               14192
156
157   DIVIDENDS DECLARED                    8000

159   TO RETAIN EARNINGS                    6192

161   # OF SHARES OUTSTANDING     160000
162   EARNINGS PER/SHR                       0.09
163   DIVIDENDS/SHR                          0.05
```

```
************************************************
*                                              *
*      BALANCE SHEET + INCOME STATEMENT         *
*              CALCULATIONS                     *
*      ------------------------------           *
*                                              *
*      ENTRIES FROM LAST OUTPUT                 *
*                                              *
*        PLANT + EQUIP AT COST    1820000       *
*        ACCUMULATED DEPRECIATION  503000       *
*        NOTES PAYABLE             150000       *
*        ACCUM. RETAINED EARNINGS  102880       *
*        BOND PAYABLE #1           200000       *
*          PAYMENT ON BOND #1       40000       *
*        BOND PAYABLE #2           280000       *
*          PAYMENT ON BOND #2       40000       *
*                                              *
*                                              *
*                                              *
*      ENTRIES FROM THIS DECISION               *
*                                              *
*        SHORT TERM INVESTMENT          0       *
*        DIVIDEND PAYMENTS/SHARE      .05       *
*        # OF SHARES OUTSTANDING   160000       *
*                                              *
*                                              *
************************************************
```

```
168                 BALANCE SHEET
           ASSETS   *************
           ------

171   CURRENT ASSETS
172     CASH                          24964
173     ACCS RECEIVABLE              855454
174     SHRT TRM INVEST                   0
175     INVENTORIES
176       RAW MATERIALS      36718
177       FINISHED GOODS    138113   174831
178         TOTAL CURR. ASSETS              1055259

180   INVESTMENTS
181     PLANT& EQUIP(CST)          1820000
182     LESS  ACCM.DEPR             594000
183       NET PLANT                        1226000
                                           -------

186         TOTAL ASSETS                   2281259
                                           -------
                                           -------
```

```
189          LIABILITIES
             -----------

191   CURRENT LIABILITY
192    NOTES PAYABLE           150000
193    EST.INC TAX PAY          14192
194    DIVIDENDS PAYABLE         8000
195       TOTAL CURR. LIABILITIES        172192

197   LONG TERM DEBT
198    BONDS PAYABLE    #1     160000
199                    #2     240000      400000
                                          ------

201      TOTAL LIABILITIES             572192

204      STOCKHOLDERS EQUITY
         -------------------

206   COMMON STOCK($10)                1600000
207   ACCUM. RET.EARN.        102880
208   ADD QTR. EARNINGS         6192     109072

210      TOTAL STK EQUITY             1709072
                                       ------

213      TOTAL LIABILITIES            2281263
         & STOCKHLDRS EQUITY
                                       ------
                                       ------
```

```
218            ANALYSIS SECTION
               ----------------


221    AVE. PRICE/UNIT      40.00
222    VAR.  COST/UNIT      25.87
223    TOTAL FIXED COST    209728

225    BREAKEVEN            14841


228    RTN ON SALES        .0636992
229    RTN ON NET WORTH    .0083037
230    RTN ON ASSETS       .0188200
231    EPS                 .0886978
232    TIMES INT. EARNED  2.950741

234    CURRENT RATIO         6.13
235    QUICK RATIO           5.11
236    DEBT/TOTAL ASSETS     0.25
237    INVENTORY TURNOVER    3.86
238    FIXED ASSET TRNOVR    0.55
239    TOTAL ASSET TRNOVR    0.30
```

© **1984 by Houghton Mifflin Company**

DECISION SHEET for TEMPOMATIC IV (DO NOT PUNCH DECIMAL POINTS; PLACE LAST DIGIT OF EACH DECISION IN RIGHT COLUMN OF BOX)

CARD 1

Column ruler: 1 2 3 4 5 6 7 8 9 10 11 12 13 14 15 16 17 18 19 20 21 22 23 24 25 26 27 28 29 30 31 32 33 34 35 36 37 38 39 40 41 42 43 44 45 46 47 48 49 50 51 52 53 54 55 56 57 58 59 60 61 62 63 64 65 66 67 68 69 70 71 72 73 74 75 76 77 78 79 80

Top labels: Company Number + 50 | Ind'y Number | Company Name | Area 3 | Area 2 | Area 1 | No. of Prod. Improvement

Row: Natl. Adv. No. Pgs. | Area 1 | Area 2 | Area 3 | Sales Price Per Unit | Number of Salespersons

Local Advertising-Number Pgs. | Number of Salespersons Hired | Area 2 | Area 3 | Area 1 | Area 2 | Area 3

CARD 2 — 02

Co. No. | Company Name | Area 3 | Area 2 | Area 1

Quarter | Number of Salespersons Discharged | Total Trfd. | Units Transferred From | Units Transferred To

CARD 3 — 03

Co. No. | A B C D E F G H I Environment Information | Cost of Environment Information | Dividend Per Share-¢ | % of Profit to Dividend | Total S-T Loan Repayment-$ | Short-Term Loan Requested-$

Area 1 | Area 2 | Area 3 | Area 1 | Area 2 | Area 3 | Plant Ordered Constructed—Units | Material Ordered—Units

CARD 4 — 04

Co. No. | A1 A2 A3 Cost | Worker Layoffs | Withdraw-$ | Deposit-$ | Short-Term Investment

Area 1 | Area 2 | Area 3 | Area 1 | Area 2 | Area 3 | Production Workers Discharged—Number | Production Workers Hired—Number | Total Actual Production—Units

CARD 5 — 05

Co. No. | Salary $/per. | Hiring $/per. | Per Crew | Crew Size | Extra Payment 1st Bond | Freq. of Pay. | Amount of Other Payment | Qtr. of 1st Payment | Amount of 1st Payment | Interest-% per yr. × 100 | Price

Salespersons | Productivity | Bonds: Issuance and Payment | Amount $ | Number | Stock Retired—Share-¢ | Min. Price | Stock Issue-Share-¢

CARD 6 — 06

Option | Co. No. | Capacity-Units | Area | Purchase Price $ | Accumulated Depreciation | Capacity-Units | Area | Sale Price $

Purchase of Plant | Sale of Plant | Material Cost: Change to ($) | Low Price | Med. Price | High Price

Reg. Pay $/Qtr. | Overtime ¢/Unit | Hiring Cost $/Person | Prod. Worker Pay: Change to ($)

© 1984 by Houghton Mifflin Company

DECISION SHEET for TEMPOMATIC IV (DO NOT PUNCH DECIMAL POINTS; PLACE LAST DIGIT OF EACH DECISION IN RIGHT COLUMN OF BOX)

CARD 1

Columns: 1 2 3 4 5 6 7 8 9 10 11 12 13 14 15 16 17 18 19 20 21 22 23 24 25 26 27 28 29 30 31 32 33 34 35 36 37 38 39 40 41 42 43 44 45 46 47 48 49 50 51 52 53 54 55 56 57 58 59 60 61 62 63 64 65 66 67 68 69 70 71 72 73 74 75 76 77 78 79 80

Natl. Adv. No. Pgs.	
Local Advertising—Number Pgs. (Area 1, Area 2, Area 3)	
No. of Prod. Improvement	
Sales Price Per Unit (Area 1, Area 2, Area 3)	
Company Name	
Ind'y Number	
Company Number + 50	

CARD 2 02

Columns: 1 2 3 4 5 6 7 8 9 10 11 12 13 14 15 16 17 18 19 20 21 22 23 24 25 26 27 28 29 30 31 32 33 34 35 36 37 38 39 40 41 42 43 44 45 46 47 48 49 50 51 52 53 54 55 56 57 58 59 60 61 62 63 64 65 66 67 68 69 70 71 72 73 74 75 76 77 78 79 80

Quarter	
Number of Salespersons Hired	
Number of Salespersons Discharged	
Number of Salespersons	
Units Transferred To (Total Trfd., Area 1, Area 2, Area 3)	
Units Transferred From	
Company Name	
Co. No.	

CARD 3 03

Columns: 1 2 3 4 5 6 7 8 9 10 11 12 13 14 15 16 17 18 19 20 21 22 23 24 25 26 27 28 29 30 31 32 33 34 35 36 37 38 39 40 41 42 43 44 45 46 47 48 49 50 51 52 53 54 55 56 57 58 59 60 61 62 63 64 65 66 67 68 69 70 71 72 73 74 75 76 77 78 79 80

Material Ordered—Units (Area 1, Area 2, Area 3)	
Plant Ordered Constructed—Units (Area 1, Area 2, Area 3)	
Short-Term Loan Requested-$	
Total S-T Loan Repayment-$	
% of Profit to Dividend	
Dividend Per Share-¢	
Cost of Environment Information	
A B C D E F G H I Environment Information	
Co. No.	

CARD 4 04

Columns: 1 2 3 4 5 6 7 8 9 10 11 12 13 14 15 16 17 18 19 20 21 22 23 24 25 26 27 28 29 30 31 32 33 34 35 36 37 38 39 40 41 42 43 44 45 46 47 48 49 50 51 52 53 54 55 56 57 58 59 60 61 62 63 64 65 66 67 68 69 70 71 72 73 74 75 76 77 78 79 80

Total Actual Production—Units (Area 1, Area 2, Area 3)	
Production Workers Hired—Number (Area 1, Area 2, Area 3)	
Production Workers Discharged—Number	
Short-Term Investment	
Deposit-$	
Withdraw-$	
Worker Layoffs (A1, A2, A3)	
Cost	
Co. No.	

CARD 5 05

Columns: 1 2 3 4 5 6 7 8 9 10 11 12 13 14 15 16 17 18 19 20 21 22 23 24 25 26 27 28 29 30 31 32 33 34 35 36 37 38 39 40 41 42 43 44 45 46 47 48 49 50 51 52 53 54 55 56 57 58 59 60 61 62 63 64 65 66 67 68 69 70 71 72 73 74 75 76 77 78 79 80

Stock Issue-Share/¢	
Number	
Stock Retired-Share/¢	
Number	
Bonds: Issuance and Payment	
Price	
Amount $	
Interest-% per yr. × 100	
Qtr. of 1st Pay.	
Amount of 1st Payment	
Freq. of Pay.	
Other Payment	
Extra Pay-ment 1st Bond	
Productivity	Salespersons
Per Crew	
Crew Size	
Salary $/per.	
Hiring $/per.	
Co. No.	

CARD 6 06

Columns: 1 2 3 4 5 6 7 8 9 10 11 12 13 14 15 16 17 18 19 20 21 22 23 24 25 26 27 28 29 30 31 32 33 34 35 36 37 38 39 40 41 42 43 44 45 46 47 48 49 50 51 52 53 54 55 56 57 58 59 60 61 62 63 64 65 66 67 68 69 70 71 72 73 74 75 76 77 78 79 80

Reg. Pay $/Qtr.	
Prod. Worker Pay: Change to ($)	
Overtime ¢/Unit	
Hiring Cost $/Person	
Material Cost: Change to ($)	
Number	
High Price	
Med. Price	
Low Price	
Min. Price	
Sale of Plant	
Sale Price $	
Accumulated Depreciation	
Purchase of Plant	
Capacity-Units	
Area	
Purchase Price $	
Capacity-Units	
Area	
Option	
Co. No.	

DECISION SHEET for TEMPOMATIC IV (DO NOT PUNCH DECIMAL POINTS; PLACE LAST DIGIT OF EACH DECISION IN RIGHT COLUMN OF BOX)

CARD 1

1 2 3 4	5 6 7 8 9 10 11 12 13 14 15 16 17 18 19 20 21 22 23 24 25 26 27 28 29 30 31 32 33 34 35 36 37 38 39 40 41 42 43 44 45 46 47 48 49 50 51 52 53 54 55 56 57 58 59 60 61 62 63 64 65 66 67 68 69 70 71 72 73 74 75 76	77 78 79 80
Natl. Adv. No. Pgs.	Area 1 / Area 2 / Area 3 — Local Advertising-Number Pgs.	Ind'y Number / Company Number + 50
	No. of Prod. Improvement — Area 1 / Area 2 / Area 3 — Sales Price Per Unit	Company Name

CARD 2

1 2 3 4	5 6 7 8 9 10 11 12 13 14 15 16 17 18 19 20 21 22 23 24 25 26 27 28 29 30 31 32 33 34 35 36 37 38 39 40 41 42 43 44 45 46 47 48 49 50 51 52 53 54 55 56 57 58 59 60 61 62 63 64 65 66 67 68 69 70 71 72 73 74 75 76	77 78 79 80	0 2
Quarter	Number of Salespersons Hired — Number of Salespersons Discharged — Area 1 / Area 2 / Area 3 — Number of Salespersons	Co. No.	
	Total Trfd. — Units Transferred To — Units Transferred From — Area 1 / Area 2 / Area 3	Company Name	

CARD 3

1 2 3 4	5 6 7 8 9 10 11 12 13 14 15 16 17 18 19 20 21 22 23 24 25 26 27 28 29 30 31 32 33 34 35 36 37 38 39 40 41 42 43 44 45 46 47 48 49 50 51 52 53 54 55 56 57 58 59 60 61 62 63 64 65 66 67 68 69 70 71 72 73 74 75 76	77 78 79 80	0 3
Area 1 / Area 2 / Area 3 — Material Ordered-Units	Short-Term Loan Requested-$ — Plant Ordered Constructed-Units — Total S-T Loan Repayment-$ — % of Profit to Dividend — Dividend Per Share-¢ — Cost of Environment Information	A B C D E F G H I Environment Information	Co. No.

CARD 4

1 2 3 4	5 6 7 8 9 10 11 12 13 14 15 16 17 18 19 20 21 22 23 24 25 26 27 28 29 30 31 32 33 34 35 36 37 38 39 40 41 42 43 44 45 46 47 48 49 50 51 52 53 54 55 56 57 58 59 60 61 62 63 64 65 66 67 68 69 70 71 72 73 74 75 76	77 78 79 80	0 4
Area 1 / Area 2 / Area 3 — Total Actual Production-Units	Production Workers Hired-Number — Area 1 / Area 2 / Area 3 — Production Workers Discharged-Number	Deposit-$ — Withdraw-$ — Short-Term Investment — A1 A2 A3 Cost — Worker Layoffs	Co. No.

CARD 5

1 2 3 4	5 6 7 8 9 10 11 12 13 14 15 16 17 18 19 20 21 22 23 24 25 26 27 28 29 30 31 32 33 34 35 36 37 38 39 40 41 42 43 44 45 46 47 48 49 50 51 52 53 54 55 56 57 58 59 60 61 62 63 64 65 66 67 68 69 70 71 72 73 74 75 76	77 78 79 80	0 5
Number — Stock Issue-Share/¢	Price — Number — Stock Retired-Share/¢ — Amount $ — Interest-% per yr. × 100 — Amount of 1st Payment — Qtr. of 1st Pay. — Freq. of Pay. — Amount of Other Payment — Extra Payment 1st Bond	Per Crew — Crew Size — Salary $/per. — Hiring $/per.	Co. No.
	Bonds: Issuance and Payment	Productivity — Salespersons	

CARD 6

1 2 3 4	5 6 7 8 9 10 11 12 13 14 15 16 17 18 19 20 21 22 23 24 25 26 27 28 29 30 31 32 33 34 35 36 37 38 39 40 41 42 43 44 45 46 47 48 49 50 51 52 53 54 55 56 57 58 59 60 61 62 63 64 65 66 67 68 69 70 71 72 73 74 75 76	77 78 79 80	0 6
Reg. Pay $/Qtr. — Overtime ¢/Unit — Hiring Cost $/Person — High Price — Med. Price — Low Price — Sale Price $ — Accumulated Depreciation — Area — Capacity-Units — Purchase Price $ — Area — Capacity-Units		Option — Co. No.
Prod. Worker Pay: Change to ($) — Material Cost: Change to ($) — Sale of Plant — Purchase of Plant		

DECISION SHEET for TEMPOMATIC IV (DO NOT PUNCH DECIMAL POINTS: PLACE LAST DIGIT OF EACH DECISION IN RIGHT COLUMN OF BOX)

CARD 1

Columns: 1 2 3 4 5 6 7 8 9 10 11 12 13 14 15 16 17 18 19 20 21 22 23 24 25 26 27 28 29 30 31 32 33 34 35 36 37 38 39 40 41 42 43 44 45 46 47 48 49 50 51 52 53 54 55 56 57 58 59 60 61 62 63 64 65 66 67 68 69 70 71 72 73 74 75 76 77 78 79 80

Natl. Adv. No. Pgs.	Area 1	Area 2	Area 3	No. of Prod. Improvement	Area 1	Area 2	Area 3	Company Name	Ind'y Number	Company Number + 50
	Local Advertising—Number Pgs.				Sales Price Per Unit					

CARD 2

Columns: 1 2 3 4 5 6 7 8 9 10 11 12 13 14 15 16 17 18 19 20 21 22 23 24 25 26 27 28 29 30 31 32 33 34 35 36 37 38 39 40 41 42 43 44 45 46 47 48 49 50 51 52 53 54 55 56 57 58 59 60 61 62 63 64 65 66 67 68 69 70 71 72 73 74 75 76 77 78 79 80 | 02

Quarter	Area 1	Area 2	Area 3	Number of Salespersons Hired	Number of Salespersons Discharged	Area 1	Area 2	Area 3	Total Trfd.	Company Name	Co. No.
		Units Transferred To					Units Transferred From				

CARD 3

Columns: 1 2 3 4 5 6 7 8 9 10 11 12 13 14 15 16 17 18 19 20 21 22 23 24 25 26 27 28 29 30 31 32 33 34 35 36 37 38 39 40 41 42 43 44 45 46 47 48 49 50 51 52 53 54 55 56 57 58 59 60 61 62 63 64 65 66 67 68 69 70 71 72 73 74 75 76 77 78 79 80 | 03

Area 1	Area 2	Area 3	Short-Term Loan Requested-$	Total S-T Loan Repayment-$	% of Profit to Dividend	Dividend Per Share-¢	Cost of Environment Information	A B C D E F G H I Environment Information	Co. No.
Material Ordered—Units		Plant Ordered Constructed—Units							

CARD 4

Columns: 1 2 3 4 5 6 7 8 9 10 11 12 13 14 15 16 17 18 19 20 21 22 23 24 25 26 27 28 29 30 31 32 33 34 35 36 37 38 39 40 41 42 43 44 45 46 47 48 49 50 51 52 53 54 55 56 57 58 59 60 61 62 63 64 65 66 67 68 69 70 71 72 73 74 75 76 77 78 79 80 | 04

Area 1	Area 2	Area 3	Area 1	Area 2	Area 3	Deposit-$	Withdraw-$	A1 A2 A3 Worker Layoffs	Cost	Co. No.
Total Actual Production—Units			Production Workers Hired—Number		Production Workers Discharged—Number		Short-Term Investment			

CARD 5

Columns: 1 2 3 4 5 6 7 8 9 10 11 12 13 14 15 16 17 18 19 20 21 22 23 24 25 26 27 28 29 30 31 32 33 34 35 36 37 38 39 40 41 42 43 44 45 46 47 48 49 50 51 52 53 54 55 56 57 58 59 60 61 62 63 64 65 66 67 68 69 70 71 72 73 74 75 76 77 78 79 80 | 05

Number	Price	Number	Amount $	Interest-% per yr. × 100	Amount of 1st Payment	Qtr. of 1st Pay.	Freq. of Pay.	Amount of Other Payment	Extra Pay- ment 1st Bond	Per Crew	Crew Size	Salary $/per.	Hiring $/per.	Co. No.
Stock Issue-Share/¢	Stock Retired-Share/¢				Bonds: Issuance and Payment					Productivity		Salespersons		

CARD 6

Columns: 1 2 3 4 5 6 7 8 9 10 11 12 13 14 15 16 17 18 19 20 21 22 23 24 25 26 27 28 29 30 31 32 33 34 35 36 37 38 39 40 41 42 43 44 45 46 47 48 49 50 51 52 53 54 55 56 57 58 59 60 61 62 63 64 65 66 67 68 69 70 71 72 73 74 75 76 77 78 79 80 | 06

Reg. Pay $/Qtr.	Overtime ¢/Unit	Hiring Cost $/Person	Number	High Price	Med. Price	Low Price	Sale Price $	Accumulated Depreciation	Area	Capacity- Units	Purchase Price $	Area	Capacity- Units	Co. No. Option
Prod. Worker Pay: Change to ($)			Stock Retired-Share/¢		Material Cost: Change to ($)		Sale of Plant				Purchase of Plant			

DECISION SHEET for TEMPOMATIC IV (DO NOT PUNCH DECIMAL POINTS; PLACE LAST DIGIT OF EACH DECISION IN RIGHT COLUMN OF BOX)

CARD 1

Column ruler: 1|2|3|4|5|6|7|8|9|10|11|12|13|14|15|16|17|18|19|20|21|22|23|24|25|26|27|28|29|30|31|32|33|34|35|36|37|38|39|40|41|42|43|44|45|46|47|48|49|50|51|52|53|54|55|56|57|58|59|60|61|62|63|64|65|66|67|68|69|70|71|72|73|74|75|76|77|78|79|80

Fields: Company Number + 50 | Ind'y Number | Company Name Area 3 | Area 2 | Sales Price Per Unit Area 1 | No. of Prod. Improvement | Area 3 | Area 2 | Area 1 | Number of Salespersons | Natl. Adv. No. Pgs. | Local Advertising—Number Pgs.

CARD 2

02

Fields: Co. No. | Company Name Area 3 | Units Transferred From Area 2 | Total Trfd. Area 1 | Units Transferred To Area 3 | Area 2 | Area 1 | Number of Salespersons Discharged | Quarter | Number of Salespersons Hired

CARD 3

03

Fields: Co. No. | A B C D E F G H I Environment Information | Cost of Environment Information | Dividend Per Share-¢ | % of Profit to Dividend | Total S-T Loan Repayment-$ | Short-Term Loan Requested-$ | Plant Ordered Constructed—Units Area 3 | Area 2 | Area 1 | Material Ordered—Units

CARD 4

04

Fields: Co. No. | Cost | A3 | A2 | A1 | Worker Layoffs | Withdraw-$ | Short-Term Investment Deposit-$ | Production Workers Discharged—Number Area 3 | Area 2 | Area 1 | Production Workers Hired—Number Area 3 | Area 2 | Area 1 | Total Actual Production—Units

CARD 5

05

Fields: Co. No. | Hiring $/per. | Salary $/per. | Crew Size | Per Crew | Extra Payment 1st Bond | Freq. of Pay. | Amount of Other Payment | Qtr. of 1st Pay. | Amount of 1st Payment | Interest-% per yr. × 100 | Amount $ | Number | Stock Retired—Share-¢ | Stock Issue—Share-¢ | Productivity | Salespersons | Bonds: Issuance and Payment

CARD 6

06

Fields: Co. No. | Capacity-Units | Area | Purchase Price $ | Area | Capacity-Units | Accumulated Depreciation | Sale Price $ | Low Price | Med. Price | High Price | Hiring Cost $/Person | Overtime ¢/Unit | Number | Reg. Pay $/Qtr. | Purchase of Plant | Sale of Plant | Material Cost: Change to ($) | Prod. Worker Pay: Change to ($)

© 1984 by Houghton Mifflin Company

DECISION SHEET for TEMPOMATIC IV (DO NOT PUNCH DECIMAL POINTS: PLACE LAST DIGIT OF EACH DECISION IN RIGHT COLUMN OF BOX)

CARD 1

Column guide: 1|2|3|4|5|6|7|8|9|10|11|12|13|14|15|16|17|18|19|20|21|22|23|24|25|26|27|28|29|30|31|32|33|34|35|36|37|38|39|40|41|42|43|44|45|46|47|48|49|50|51|52|53|54|55|56|57|58|59|60|61|62|63|64|65|66|67|68|69|70|71|72|73|74|75|76|77|78|79|80

Natl. Adv. No. Pgs.	Area 1	Area 2	Area 3	No. of Prod. Improvement	Area 1	Area 2	Area 3	Company Name	Ind'y Number	Company Number + 50
	Local Advertising-Number Pgs.				Sales Price Per Unit					

CARD 2 02

Quarter	Area 1	Area 2	Area 3	Number of Salespersons Hired	Area 1	Area 2	Area 3	Company Name	Co. No.
	Number of Salespersons Discharged		Number of Salespersons		Units Transferred To	Total Trfd.	Units Transferred From		

CARD 3 03

Area 1	Area 2	Area 3	Area 1	Area 2	Area 3	Short-Term Loan Requested-$	Total S-T Loan Repayment-$	% of Profit to Dividend	Dividend Per Share-¢	Cost of Environment Information	A B C D E F G H I Environment Information	Co. No.
Material Ordered-Units			Plant Ordered Constructed-Units									

CARD 4 04

Area 1	Area 2	Area 3	Area 1	Area 2	Area 3	Deposit-$	Withdraw-$	A1 A2 A3 Worker Layoffs	Cost	Co. No.
Total Actual Production-Units			Production Workers Hired-Number			Short-Term Investment		Production Workers Discharged-Number		

CARD 5 05

Number	Price	Amount $	Interest-% per yr. × 100	Amount of 1st Payment	Qtr. of 1st Pay.	Amount of Other Payment	Freq. of Pay.	Extra Payment 1st Bond	Per Crew	Crew Size	Salary $/per.	Hiring $/per.	Co. No.
Stock Retired-Share/¢						Bonds: Issuance and Payment			Productivity		Salespersons		

CARD 6 06

Number	Min. Price	Hiring Cost $/Person	High Price	Med. Price	Low Price	Sale Price $	Accumulated Depreciation	Area	Capacity-Units	Purchase Price $	Area	Capacity-Units	Option	Co. No.
Stock Issue-Share/¢	Overtime ¢/Unit				Material Cost: Change to ($)	Sale of Plant				Purchase of Plant				

Reg. Pay $/Qtr.

Prod. Worker Pay: Change to ($)

DECISION SHEET for TEMPOMATIC IV (DO NOT PUNCH DECIMAL POINTS; PLACE LAST DIGIT OF EACH DECISION IN RIGHT COLUMN OF BOX)

CARD 1

Columns: 1 2 3 4 | 5 6 7 8 9 |10|11|12|13|14|15|16|17|18|19|20|21|22|23|24|25|26|27|28|29|30|31|32|33|34|35|36|37|38|39|40|41|42|43|44|45|46|47|48|49|50|51|52|53|54|55|56|57|58|59|60|61|62|63|64|65|66|67|68|69|70|71|72|73|74|75|76|77|78|79|80

Natl. Adv. No. Pgs.	Area 1	Area 2	Area 3	No. of Prod. Improvement	Area 1	Area 2	Area 3	Ind'v Number	Company Number + 50
	Local Advertising-Number Pgs.				Sales Price Per Unit				

CARD 2

Quarter	Number of Salespersons Hired	Area 1	Area 2	Area 3	Total Trfd.	Area 1	Area 2	Area 3	Company Name	Co. No.	02
	Number of Salespersons Discharged	Number of Salespersons			Units Transferred To	Units Transferred From					

CARD 3

Area 1	Area 2	Area 3	Short-Term Loan Requested-$	Total S-T Loan Repayment-$	% of Profit to Dividend	Dividend Per Share-¢	Cost of Environment Information	A B C D E F G H I Environment Information	Co. No.	03
Material Ordered-Units		Plant Ordered Constructed-Units								

CARD 4

Area 1	Area 2	Area 3	Area 1	Area 2	Area 3	Deposit-$	Withdraw-$	A1 A2 A3 Cost	Worker Layoffs	Co. No.	04
Total Actual Production-Units		Production Workers Hired-Number		Production Workers Discharged-Number		Short-Term Investment					

CARD 5

Amount $	Interest-% per yr. X 100	Amount of 1st Payment	Qtr. of 1st Pay.	Amount of Other Payment	Freq. of Pay.	Extra Payment 1st Bond	Per Crew	Crew Size	Salary $/per.	Hiring $/per.	Co. No.	05
Stock Retired-Share/¢	Number		Bonds: Issuance and Payment				Productivity		Salespersons			

CARD 6

Overtime ¢/Unit	Hiring Cost $/Person	High Price	Med. Price	Low Price	Sale Price $	Accumulated Depreciation	Capacity-Units	Area	Purchase Price $	Area	Capacity-Units	Co. No.	06
Reg. Pay $/Qtr.	Stock Issue-Share/¢	Min. Price		Material Cost: Change to ($)		Sale of Plant			Purchase of Plant				Option

Prod. Worker Pay: Change to ($)

DECISION SHEET for TEMPOMATIC IV (DO NOT PUNCH DECIMAL POINTS: PLACE LAST DIGIT OF EACH DECISION IN RIGHT COLUMN OF BOX)

CARD 1

Natl. Adv. No. Pgs.	Area 1	Area 2	Area 3	No. of Prod. Improvement	Area 1	Area 2	Area 3	Company Name	Ind'y Number	Company Number + 50
	Local Advertising–Number Pgs.				Sales Price Per Unit					

CARD 2

Co. No. 02

Quarter	Number of Salespersons Hired	Number of Salespersons Discharged	Area 1	Area 2	Area 3	Total Trfd.	Area 1	Area 2	Area 3	Company Name
			Number of Salespersons				Units Transferred To		Units Transferred From	

CARD 3

Co. No. 03

Area 1	Area 2	Area 3	Short-Term Loan Requested–$	Total S-T Loan Repayment–$	% of Profit to Dividend	Dividend Per Share–¢	Cost of Environment Information	A B C D E F G H I Environment Information
Material Ordered–Units			Plant Ordered Constructed–Units					

CARD 4

Co. No. 04

Area 1	Area 2	Area 3	Area 1	Area 2	Area 3	Deposit–$ Short-Term Investment	Withdraw–$	A1	A2	A3	Cost
Total Actual Production–Units			Production Workers Hired–Number	Production Workers Discharged–Number				Worker Layoffs			

CARD 5

Co. No. 05

Number	Min. Price	Number	Price	Amount $	Interest–% per yr. X 100	Amount of 1st Payment	Qtr. of 1st Pay.	Freq. of Pay.	Amount of Other Payment	Extra Pay-ment 1st Bond	Per Crew	Crew Size	Salary $/per.	Hiring $/per.
Stock Issue–Share/¢		Stock Retired–Share/¢				Bonds: Issuance and Payment					Productivity		Salespersons	

CARD 6

Option 06

Reg. Pay $/Qtr.	Overtime ¢/Unit	Hiring Cost $/Person	High Price	Med. Price	Low Price	Sale Price $	Accumulated Depreciation	Area	Purchase Price $	Area	Capacity-Units
Prod. Worker Pay: Change to ($)			Material Cost: Change to ($)			Sale of Plant			Purchase of Plant		

© 1984 by Houghton Mifflin Company

DECISION SHEET for TEMPOMATIC IV (DO NOT PUNCH DECIMAL POINTS: PLACE LAST DIGIT OF EACH DECISION IN RIGHT COLUMN OF BOX)

CARD 1

| 1 | 2 | 3 | 4 | 5 | 6 | 7 | 8 | 9 |10|11|12|13|14|15|16|17|18|19|20|21|22|23|24|25|26|27|28|29|30|31|32|33|34|35|36|37|38|39|40|41|42|43|44|45|46|47|48|49|50|51|52|53|54|55|56|57|58|59|60|61|62|63|64|65|66|67|68|69|70|71|72|73|74|75|76|77|78|79|80 |

Natl. Adv. No. Pgs. — Area 1 — Area 2 — Area 3 : Local Advertising-Number Pgs.
No. of Prod. Improvement
Area 1 — Area 2 — Area 3 : Sales Price Per Unit
Ind'y Number — Company Name — Company Number + 50

CARD 2

| 1 | 2 | 3 | 4 | 5 | 6 | 7 | 8 | 9 |10|11|12|13|14|15|16|17|18|19|20|21|22|23|24|25|26|27|28|29|30|31|32|33|34|35|36|37|38|39|40|41|42|43|44|45|46|47|48|49|50|51|52|53|54|55|56|57|58|59|60|61|62|63|64|65|66|67|68|69|70|71|72|73|74|75|76|77|78|79|80 |

Quarter
Number of Salespersons Hired — Number of Salespersons Discharged : Number of Salespersons
Area 1 — Area 2 — Area 3 : Units Transferred To — Total Trfd. — Area 1 — Area 2 — Area 3 : Units Transferred From
Company Name — Co. No. — 02

CARD 3

| 1 | 2 | 3 | 4 | 5 | 6 | 7 | 8 | 9 |10|11|12|13|14|15|16|17|18|19|20|21|22|23|24|25|26|27|28|29|30|31|32|33|34|35|36|37|38|39|40|41|42|43|44|45|46|47|48|49|50|51|52|53|54|55|56|57|58|59|60|61|62|63|64|65|66|67|68|69|70|71|72|73|74|75|76|77|78|79|80 |

Area 1 — Area 2 — Area 3 : Material Ordered-Units
Plant Ordered Constructed-Units
Short-Term Loan Requested-$
Total S-T Loan Repayment-$
% of Profit to Dividend — Dividend Per Share-¢
Cost of Environment Information — A B C D E F G H I : Environment Information — Co. No. — 03

CARD 4

| 1 | 2 | 3 | 4 | 5 | 6 | 7 | 8 | 9 |10|11|12|13|14|15|16|17|18|19|20|21|22|23|24|25|26|27|28|29|30|31|32|33|34|35|36|37|38|39|40|41|42|43|44|45|46|47|48|49|50|51|52|53|54|55|56|57|58|59|60|61|62|63|64|65|66|67|68|69|70|71|72|73|74|75|76|77|78|79|80 |

Area 1 — Area 2 — Area 3 : Total Actual Production-Units
Production Workers Hired-Number
Production Workers Discharged-Number
Deposit-$ — Withdraw-$: Short-Term Investment
A1 A2 A3 — Cost : Worker Layoffs — Co. No. — 04

CARD 5

| 1 | 2 | 3 | 4 | 5 | 6 | 7 | 8 | 9 |10|11|12|13|14|15|16|17|18|19|20|21|22|23|24|25|26|27|28|29|30|31|32|33|34|35|36|37|38|39|40|41|42|43|44|45|46|47|48|49|50|51|52|53|54|55|56|57|58|59|60|61|62|63|64|65|66|67|68|69|70|71|72|73|74|75|76|77|78|79|80 |

Number — Stock Issue-Share/¢ : Price — Amount $
Number — Stock Retired-Share/¢ : Interest-% per yr. X 100 — Amount of 1st Payment — Qtr. of 1st Pay. — Freq. of Pay. — Amount of Other Payment : Bonds: Issuance and Payment
Extra Pay-ment 1st Bond
Productivity — Per Crew — Crew Size — Salary $/per. — Hiring $/per. : Salespersons — Co. No. — 05

CARD 6

| 1 | 2 | 3 | 4 | 5 | 6 | 7 | 8 | 9 |10|11|12|13|14|15|16|17|18|19|20|21|22|23|24|25|26|27|28|29|30|31|32|33|34|35|36|37|38|39|40|41|42|43|44|45|46|47|48|49|50|51|52|53|54|55|56|57|58|59|60|61|62|63|64|65|66|67|68|69|70|71|72|73|74|75|76|77|78|79|80 |

Reg. Pay $/Qtr. — Overtime ¢/Unit — Hiring Cost $/Person : Prod. Worker Pay: Change to ($)
Number — Min. Price — High Price — Med. Price — Low Price — Sale Price $: Material Cost: Change to ($) — Sale of Plant
Accumulated Depreciation — Area : Purchase Price $ — Capacity-Units — Area : Purchase of Plant — Capacity-Units — Option — Co. No. — 06

© 1984 by Houghton Mifflin Company

DECISION SHEET for TEMPOMATIC IV (DO NOT PUNCH DECIMAL POINTS; PLACE LAST DIGIT OF EACH DECISION IN RIGHT COLUMN OF BOX)

CARD 1

| 1|2|3|4 | 5|6|7 | 8|9|10|11|12|13|14|15|16|17|18|19|20|21|22|23|24|25|26|27|28|29|30|31|32|33|34|35|36|37|38|39|40|41|42|43|44|45|46|47|48|49|50|51|52|53|54|55|56|57|58|59|60|61|62|63|64|65|66|67|68|69|70|71|72|73|74|75|76|77|78|79|80 |

Natl. Adv. No. Pgs. — Area 1 — Area 2 — Area 3 — Local Advertising–Number Pgs. — No. of Prod. Improvement — Area 1 — Area 2 — Area 3 — Sales Price Per Unit — Company Name — Ind'y Number — Company Number + 50

CARD 2

02

Quarter — Number of Salespersons Hired — Number of Salespersons Discharged — Area 1 — Area 2 — Area 3 — Number of Salespersons — Area 1 — Area 2 — Area 3 — Units Transferred To — Total Trfd. — Units Transferred From — Company Name — Co. No.

CARD 3

03

Area 1 — Area 2 — Area 3 — Material Ordered–Units — Plant Ordered Constructed–Units — Short-Term Loan Requested–$ — Total S-T Loan Repayment–$ — % of Profit to Dividend — Dividend Per Share–¢ — Cost of Environment Information — A B C D E F G H I — Environment Information — Co. No.

CARD 4

04

Area 1 — Area 2 — Area 3 — Total Actual Production–Units — Production Workers Hired–Number — Area 1 — Area 2 — Area 3 — Production Workers Discharged–Number — Deposit–$ — Withdraw–$ — Short-Term Investment — A1 A2 A3 — Worker Layoffs — Cost — Co. No.

CARD 5

05

Number — Stock Issue-Share/¢ — Price — Stock Retired-Share/¢ — Amount $ — Interest-% per yr. × 100 — Amount of 1st Payment — Qtr. of 1st Pay. — Freq. of Pay. — Amount of Other Payment — Extra Payment 1st Bond — Bonds: Issuance and Payment — Per Crew — Crew Size — Salary $/per. — Hiring $/per. — Productivity — Salespersons — Co. No.

CARD 6

06

Reg. Pay $/Qtr. — Overtime ¢/Unit — Hiring Cost $/Person — Prod. Worker Pay: Change to ($) — High Price — Med. Price — Low Price — Material Cost: Change to ($) — Sale Price $ — Accumulated Depreciation — Sale of Plant — Purchase Price $ — Capacity-Units — Area — Purchase of Plant — Capacity-Units — Option — Co. No.

©1984 by Houghton Mifflin Company

DECISION SHEET for TEMPOMATIC IV (DO NOT PUNCH DECIMAL POINTS; PLACE LAST DIGIT OF EACH DECISION IN RIGHT COLUMN OF BOX)

CARD 1

Columns: 1 2 3 4 | 5 | 6 | 7 | 8 | 9 |10|11|12|13|14|15|16|17|18|19|20|21|22|23|24|25|26|27|28|29|30|31|32|33|34|35|36|37|38|39|40|41|42|43|44|45|46|47|48|49|50|51|52|53|54|55|56|57|58|59|60|61|62|63|64|65|66|67|68|69|70|71|72|73|74|75|76|77|78|79|80

- Natl. Adv. No. Pgs.
- Local Advertising-Number Pgs.: Area 1, Area 2, Area 3
- No. of Prod. Improvement
- Sales Price Per Unit: Area 1, Area 2, Area 3
- Ind'y Number
- Company Number + 50

CARD 2

- Number of Salespersons Hired: Area 1, Area 2, Area 3
- Number of Salespersons Discharged
- Number of Salespersons
- Units Transferred To
- Units Transferred From
- Total Trfd.: Area 1, Area 2, Area 3
- Company Name
- Co. No.
- 0 2

CARD 3

- Material Ordered—Units: Area 1, Area 2, Area 3
- Plant Ordered Constructed—Units
- Short-Term Loan Requested-$
- Total S-T Loan Repayment-$
- % of Profit to Dividend
- Dividend Per Share-¢
- Cost of Environment Information
- Environment Information: A B C D E F G H I
- Co. No.
- 0 3

CARD 4

- Total Actual Production—Units: Area 1, Area 2, Area 3
- Production Workers Hired—Number
- Production Workers Discharged—Number
- Worker Layoffs
- Short-Term Investment
- Deposit-$
- Withdraw-$
- Cost: A1 A2 A3
- Co. No.
- 0 4

CARD 5

- Stock Issue-Share/¢
- Stock Retired-Share/¢
- Bonds: Issuance and Payment
- Amount $
- Interest-% per yr. X 100
- Amount of 1st Payment
- Qtr. of 1st Pay.
- Freq. of Pay.
- Amount of Other Payment
- Extra Payment 1st Bond
- Productivity
- Per Crew
- Crew Size
- Salary $/per.
- Salespersons
- Hiring $/Per
- Co. No.
- 0 5

CARD 6

- Prod. Worker Pay: Change to ($)
- Reg. Pay $/Qtr.
- Overtime ¢/Unit
- Hiring Cost $/Person
- Material Cost: Change to ($)
- Sale of Plant
- High Price
- Med. Price
- Low Price
- Sale Price $
- Accumulated Depreciation
- Purchase Price $
- Purchase of Plant
- Capacity-Units
- Area
- Capacity-Units
- Option
- Co. No.
- 0 6

ENVIRONMENT INFORMATION FORM

Company _____   Quarter _____

Circle column number of information desired and transfer cost to the last column.

	Cost of information	Cost to company	

67 Sales potential, in units, for four quarters in advance

Quarter	Area 1	Area 2	Area 3

Cost of information: **$25,000** — 67

68 Sales potential, in units, for one quarter only (one of the next four quarters)   Quarter _____
Area 1_____ Area 2 _____ Area 3 _____

Cost of information: **$7,500** — 68

69 Number of salespersons in industry this quarter
Area 1 _____ Area 2 _____ Area 3 _____

Cost of information: **$2,000** — 69

70 Plant capacity, in product units, for industry this quarter

	Area 1	Area 2	Area 3
Present			
Under construction			
Ordered this quarter			

Cost of information: **$3,000** — 70

71 Number of pages of national advertising this quarter   Total _____

Cost of information: **$1,500** — 71

72 Number of pages of local advertising this quarter
Area 1 _____ Area 2 _____ Area 3 _____

Cost of information: **$1,500** — 72

73 Sales, by company, this quarter

Co. #	Units	Co. #	Units	Co. #	Units
1		5		9	
2		6		10	
3		7		11	
4		8		12	

Cost of information: **$3,000** — 73

74 Sales price, by company, this quarter

Co. #	Price	Co. #	Price	Co. #	Price
1		5		9	
2		6		10	
3		7		11	
4		8		12	

Cost of information: **$2,000** — 74

75 News bulletin _____

_____

_____

_____

Cost of information: **$1,000** — 75

TOTAL cost of environment survey report

ENVIRONMENT INFORMATION FORM

Company _____   Quarter _____

Circle column number of information desired and transfer cost to the last column.

	Cost of information	Cost to company	

67   Sales potential, in units, for four quarters in advance $25,000   67

Quarter	Area 1	Area 2	Area 3

68   Sales potential, in units, for one quarter only (one of the next four quarters)   Quarter _____ $7,500   68
Area 1_____ Area 2 _____ Area 3 _____

69   Number of salespersons in industry this quarter $2,000   69
Area 1 _____ Area 2 _____ Area 3 _____

70   Plant capacity, in product units, for industry this quarter $3,000   70

	Area 1	Area 2	Area 3
Present			
Under construction			
Ordered this quarter			

71   Number of pages of national advertising this quarter   Total _____ $1,500   71

72   Number of pages of local advertising this quarter $1,500   72
Area 1 _____ Area 2 _____ Area 3 _____

73   Sales, by company, this quarter $3,000   73

Co. #	Units	Co. #	Units	Co. #	Units
1		5		9	
2		6		10	
3		7		11	
4		8		12	

74   Sales price, by company, this quarter $2,000   74

Co. #	Price	Co. #	Price	Co. #	Price
1		5		9	
2		6		10	
3		7		11	
4		8		12	

75   News bulletin _____ $1,000   75

_____

_____

_____

TOTAL cost of environment survey report

ENVIRONMENT INFORMATION FORM

Company _____   Quarter _____

Circle column number of information desired and transfer cost to the last column.

		Cost of information	Cost to company	
67	Sales potential, in units, for four quarters in advance	$25,000		67

Quarter	Area 1	Area 2	Area 3

68 Sales potential, in units, for one quarter only (one of the next four quarters)   Quarter _____
Area 1 _____ Area 2 _____ Area 3 _____ $7,500   68

69 Number of salespersons in industry this quarter
Area 1 _____ Area 2 _____ Area 3 _____ $2,000   69

70 Plant capacity, in product units, for industry this quarter $3,000   70

	Area 1	Area 2	Area 3
Present			
Under construction			
Ordered this quarter			

71 Number of pages of national advertising this quarter   Total _____ $1,500   71

72 Number of pages of local advertising this quarter
Area 1 _____ Area 2 _____ Area 3 _____ $1,500   72

73 Sales, by company, this quarter $3,000   73

Co. #	Units	Co. #	Units	Co. #	Units
1		5		9	
2		6		10	
3		7		11	
4		8		12	

74 Sales price, by company, this quarter $2,000   74

Co. #	Price	Co. #	Price	Co. #	Price
1		5		9	
2		6		10	
3		7		11	
4		8		12	

75 News bulletin _____ $1,000   75

_____

_____

_____

_____

TOTAL cost of environment survey report

ENVIRONMENT INFORMATION FORM

Company _____   Quarter _____

Circle column number of information desired and transfer cost to the last column.

		Cost of information	Cost to company	

67 Sales potential, in units, for four quarters in advance

Quarter	Area 1	Area 2	Area 3

Cost of information: $25,000   67

68 Sales potential, in units, for one quarter only (one of the next
   four quarters)   Quarter _____
Area 1_____ Area 2 _____ Area 3 _____

Cost of information: $7,500   68

69 Number of salespersons in industry this quarter
Area 1 _____ Area 2 _____ Area 3 _____

Cost of information: $2,000   69

70 Plant capacity, in product units, for industry this quarter

	Area 1	Area 2	Area 3
Present			
Under construction			
Ordered this quarter			

Cost of information: $3,000   70

71 Number of pages of national advertising this quarter   Total _____

Cost of information: $1,500   71

72 Number of pages of local advertising this quarter
Area 1 _____ Area 2 _____ Area 3 _____

Cost of information: $1,500   72

73 Sales, by company, this quarter

Co. #	Units	Co. #	Units	Co. #	Units
1		5		9	
2		6		10	
3		7		11	
4		8		12	

Cost of information: $3,000   73

74 Sales price, by company, this quarter

Co. #	Price	Co. #	Price	Co. #	Price
1		5		9	
2		6		10	
3		7		11	
4		8		12	

Cost of information: $2,000   74

75 News bulletin _____

_____

_____

_____

Cost of information: $1,000   75

TOTAL cost of environment survey report

ENVIRONMENT INFORMATION FORM

Company _____   Quarter _____

Circle column number of information desired and transfer cost to the last column.

	Cost of information	Cost to company	
67 Sales potential, in units, for four quarters in advance	$25,000		67

Quarter	Area 1	Area 2	Area 3

	Cost of information	Cost to company	
68 Sales potential, in units, for one quarter only (one of the next four quarters) Quarter _____ Area 1_____ Area 2 _____ Area 3 _____	$7,500		68
69 Number of salespersons in industry this quarter Area 1 _____ Area 2 _____ Area 3 _____	$2,000		69
70 Plant capacity, in product units, for industry this quarter	$3,000		70

	Area 1	Area 2	Area 3
Present			
Under construction			
Ordered this quarter			

	Cost of information	Cost to company	
71 Number of pages of national advertising this quarter Total _____	$1,500		71
72 Number of pages of local advertising this quarter Area 1 _____ Area 2 _____ Area 3 _____	$1,500		72
73 Sales, by company, this quarter	$3,000		73

Co. #	Units	Co. #	Units	Co. #	Units
1		5		9	
2		6		10	
3		7		11	
4		8		12	

	Cost of information	Cost to company	
74 Sales price, by company, this quarter	$2,000		74

Co. #	Price	Co. #	Price	Co. #	Price
1		5		9	
2		6		10	
3		7		11	
4		8		12	

	Cost of information	Cost to company	
75 News bulletin _____	$1,000		75

_____

_____

_____

TOTAL cost of environment survey report

ENVIRONMENT INFORMATION FORM

Company _____   Quarter _____

Circle column number of information desired and transfer cost to the last column.

					Cost of information	Cost to company	

67   Sales potential, in units, for four quarters in advance $25,000   67

Quarter	Area 1	Area 2	Area 3

68   Sales potential, in units, for one quarter only (one of the next four quarters)   Quarter _____ $7,500   68
Area 1_____ Area 2 _____ Area 3 _____

69   Number of salespersons in industry this quarter $2,000   69
Area 1 _____ Area 2 _____ Area 3 _____

70   Plant capacity, in product units, for industry this quarter $3,000   70

	Area 1	Area 2	Area 3
Present			
Under construction			
Ordered this quarter			

71   Number of pages of national advertising this quarter   Total _____ $1,500   71

72   Number of pages of local advertising this quarter $1,500   72
Area 1 _____ Area 2 _____ Area 3 _____

73   Sales, by company, this quarter $3,000   73

Co. #	Units	Co. #	Units	Co. #	Units
1		5		9	
2		6		10	
3		7		11	
4		8		12	

74   Sales price, by company, this quarter $2,000   74

Co. #	Price	Co. #	Price	Co. #	Price
1		5		9	
2		6		10	
3		7		11	
4		8		12	

75   News bulletin _____ $1,000   75

_____

_____

_____

_____

TOTAL cost of environment survey report

ENVIRONMENT INFORMATION FORM

Company _____   Quarter _____

Circle column number of information desired and transfer cost to the last column.

		Cost of information	Cost to company	

67 Sales potential, in units, for four quarters in advance

Quarter	Area 1	Area 2	Area 3

Cost of information: $25,000 — 67

68 Sales potential, in units, for one quarter only (one of the next four quarters)   Quarter _____
Area 1 _____ Area 2 _____ Area 3 _____

Cost of information: $7,500 — 68

69 Number of salespersons in industry this quarter
Area 1 _____ Area 2 _____ Area 3 _____

Cost of information: $2,000 — 69

70 Plant capacity, in product units, for industry this quarter

	Area 1	Area 2	Area 3
Present			
Under construction			
Ordered this quarter			

Cost of information: $3,000 — 70

71 Number of pages of national advertising this quarter   Total _____

Cost of information: $1,500 — 71

72 Number of pages of local advertising this quarter
Area 1 _____ Area 2 _____ Area 3 _____

Cost of information: $1,500 — 72

73 Sales, by company, this quarter

Co. #	Units	Co. #	Units	Co. #	Units
1		5		9	
2		6		10	
3		7		11	
4		8		12	

Cost of information: $3,000 — 73

74 Sales price, by company, this quarter

Co. #	Price	Co. #	Price	Co. #	Price
1		5		9	
2		6		10	
3		7		11	
4		8		12	

Cost of information: $2,000 — 74

75 News bulletin _____

Cost of information: $1,000 — 75

_____

_____

_____

TOTAL cost of environment survey report

ENVIRONMENT INFORMATION FORM

Company _____   Quarter _____

Circle column number of information desired and transfer cost to the last column.

		Cost of information	Cost to company	

67   Sales potential, in units, for four quarters in advance

Quarter	Area 1	Area 2	Area 3

$25,000   67

68   Sales potential, in units, for one quarter only (one of the next
four quarters)   Quarter _____
Area 1 _____ Area 2 _____ Area 3 _____

$7,500   68

69   Number of salespersons in industry this quarter
Area 1 _____ Area 2 _____ Area 3 _____

$2,000   69

70   Plant capacity, in product units, for industry this quarter

	Area 1	Area 2	Area 3
Present			
Under construction			
Ordered this quarter			

$3,000   70

71   Number of pages of national advertising this quarter   Total _____

$1,500   71

72   Number of pages of local advertising this quarter
Area 1 _____ Area 2 _____ Area 3 _____

$1,500   72

73   Sales, by company, this quarter

Co. #	Units	Co. #	Units	Co. #	Units
1		5		9	
2		6		10	
3		7		11	
4		8		12	

$3,000   73

74   Sales price, by company, this quarter

Co. #	Price	Co. #	Price	Co. #	Price
1		5		9	
2		6		10	
3		7		11	
4		8		12	

$2,000   74

75   News bulletin _____

_____

_____

_____

$1,000   75

TOTAL cost of environment survey report

ENVIRONMENT INFORMATION FORM

Company _____   Quarter _____

Circle column number of information desired and transfer cost to the last column.

	Cost of information	Cost to company	

67 Sales potential, in units, for four quarters in advance

Quarter	Area 1	Area 2	Area 3

Cost of information: $25,000 — 67

68 Sales potential, in units, for one quarter only (one of the next four quarters)   Quarter _____
Area 1_____ Area 2 _____ Area 3 _____

Cost of information: $7,500 — 68

69 Number of salespersons in industry this quarter
Area 1 _____ Area 2 _____ Area 3 _____

Cost of information: $2,000 — 69

70 Plant capacity, in product units, for industry this quarter

	Area 1	Area 2	Area 3
Present			
Under construction			
Ordered this quarter			

Cost of information: $3,000 — 70

71 Number of pages of national advertising this quarter   Total _____

Cost of information: $1,500 — 71

72 Number of pages of local advertising this quarter
Area 1 _____ Area 2 _____ Area 3 _____

Cost of information: $1,500 — 72

73 Sales, by company, this quarter

Co. #	Units	Co. #	Units	Co. #	Units
1		5		9	
2		6		10	
3		7		11	
4		8		12	

Cost of information: $3,000 — 73

74 Sales price, by company, this quarter

Co. #	Price	Co. #	Price	Co. #	Price
1		5		9	
2		6		10	
3		7		11	
4		8		12	

Cost of information: $2,000 — 74

75 News bulletin _____

_____

_____

_____

Cost of information: $1,000 — 75

TOTAL cost of environment survey report

ENVIRONMENT INFORMATION FORM

Company _____   Quarter _____

Circle column number of information desired and transfer cost to the last column.

	Cost of information	Cost to company	

67 Sales potential, in units, for four quarters in advance — $25,000 — 67

Quarter	Area 1	Area 2	Area 3

68 Sales potential, in units, for one quarter only (one of the next four quarters)   Quarter _____
Area 1_____ Area 2 _____ Area 3 _____ $7,500 — 68

69 Number of salespersons in industry this quarter $2,000 — 69
Area 1 _____ Area 2 _____ Area 3 _____

70 Plant capacity, in product units, for industry this quarter $3,000 — 70

	Area 1	Area 2	Area 3
Present			
Under construction			
Ordered this quarter			

71 Number of pages of national advertising this quarter   Total _____ $1,500 — 71

72 Number of pages of local advertising this quarter $1,500 — 72
Area 1 _____ Area 2 _____ Area 3 _____

73 Sales, by company, this quarter $3,000 — 73

Co. #	Units	Co. #	Units	Co. #	Units
1		5		9	
2		6		10	
3		7		11	
4		8		12	

74 Sales price, by company, this quarter $2,000 — 74

Co. #	Price	Co. #	Price	Co. #	Price
1		5		9	
2		6		10	
3		7		11	
4		8		12	

75 News bulletin _____ $1,000 — 75

_____

_____

_____

TOTAL cost of environment survey report

ENVIRONMENT INFORMATION FORM

Company _____   Quarter _____

Circle column number of information desired and transfer cost to the last column.

		Cost of information	Cost to company	

67   Sales potential, in units, for four quarters in advance

Quarter	Area 1	Area 2	Area 3

$25,000 — 67

68   Sales potential, in units, for one quarter only (one of the next
       four quarters)   Quarter _____
       Area 1 _____ Area 2 _____ Area 3 _____

$7,500 — 68

69   Number of salespersons in industry this quarter
       Area 1 _____ Area 2 _____ Area 3 _____

$2,000 — 69

70   Plant capacity, in product units, for industry this quarter

	Area 1	Area 2	Area 3
Present			
Under construction			
Ordered this quarter			

$3,000 — 70

71   Number of pages of national advertising this quarter   Total _____

$1,500 — 71

72   Number of pages of local advertising this quarter
       Area 1 _____ Area 2 _____ Area 3 _____

$1,500 — 72

73   Sales, by company, this quarter

Co. #	Units	Co. #	Units	Co. #	Units
1		5		9	
2		6		10	
3		7		11	
4		8		12	

$3,000 — 73

74   Sales price, by company, this quarter

Co. #	Price	Co. #	Price	Co. #	Price
1		5		9	
2		6		10	
3		7		11	
4		8		12	

$2,000 — 74

75   News bulletin _____

$1,000 — 75

_____

_____

_____

TOTAL cost of environment survey report

ENVIRONMENT INFORMATION FORM

Company _____   Quarter _____

Circle column number of information desired and transfer cost to the last column.

	Cost of information	Cost to company	

67   Sales potential, in units, for four quarters in advance   — $25,000 — 67

Quarter	Area 1	Area 2	Area 3

68   Sales potential, in units, for one quarter only (one of the next four quarters)   Quarter _____   — $7,500 — 68
Area 1 _____   Area 2 _____   Area 3 _____

69   Number of salespersons in industry this quarter   — $2,000 — 69
Area 1 _____   Area 2 _____   Area 3 _____

70   Plant capacity, in product units, for industry this quarter   — $3,000 — 70

	Area 1	Area 2	Area 3
Present			
Under construction			
Ordered this quarter			

71   Number of pages of national advertising this quarter   Total _____   — $1,500 — 71

72   Number of pages of local advertising this quarter   — $1,500 — 72
Area 1 _____   Area 2 _____   Area 3 _____

73   Sales, by company, this quarter   — $3,000 — 73

Co. #	Units	Co. #	Units	Co. #	Units
1		5		9	
2		6		10	
3		7		11	
4		8		12	

74   Sales price, by company, this quarter   — $2,000 — 74

Co. #	Price	Co. #	Price	Co. #	Price
1		5		9	
2		6		10	
3		7		11	
4		8		12	

75   News bulletin _____   — $1,000 — 75

_____

_____

_____

TOTAL cost of environment survey report

Index